Variations on a Theme

Upcoming Civil War Non-Fiction

SPIES OF THE MISSISSIPPI
*Confederate Secret Service Operations
in the Trans-Mississippi*
by D. H. Rule and G. E. Rule

GRATIOT STREET PRISON
Union Civil War Prison in St. Louis
by D. H. Rule

TUCKER'S WAR
Missouri and the Northwest Conspiracy
by G. E. Rule

SULTANA:

A Case For Sabotage

by
D. H. Rule

Variations *on a Theme*
Private Label Publishing

VARIATIONS ON A THEME LLC
Private Label Publishing
variationspublishing.com

Sultana: A Case For Sabotage

A Variations on a Theme book/published by arrangement with the author

Publishing history: *Sultana: A Case For Sabotage* original article copyright ©2000 Debra Houdek Rule; published in *North & South Magazine*, Volume 5, Number 1, December 2001

ISBN: 978-1-940058-05-4

To the brave Americans of
United Flight 93, who gave their lives for
our nation at Shanksville, Pennsylvania
September 11, 2001.

Contents

Introduction

The war didn't end when Lee surrendered. That's a myth that's grown up over time. General Lee didn't, and couldn't, surrender the Confederacy. It wasn't all sunshine and peace, with everything forgiven and forgotten the next day after Appomattox. Lee surrendered the Army of Northern Virginia on April 9, 1865, and yet the war continued. President Lincoln was shot the night of April 14, 1865, and the war continued.

On April 25, 1865, Colonel James H. Baker, Provost Marshal of the Union Department of Missouri, issued his first report on the Confederate Boatburners working under Joseph W. Tucker. A later, updated, version of Baker's report would be included in the trials of the Lincoln conspirators. Colonel Baker sent out urgent letters and reports, hunting for a man named Robert Louden, an escaped Boatburner under sentence of death in St. Louis. And the war continued.

The steamer *Sultana* exploded and burned on the Mississippi River in the early morning hours of April 27, 1865, killing over seventeen hundred people, most of them Union POWs returning home from the prison camps of the south, and the war continued. The very night *Sultana* left Memphis, Missouri was preparing for an expected invasion from Arkansas. Guerilla bands patrolled the river area across from Memphis.

Just days after *Sultana* was destroyed the Confederate Department of the Trans-Mississippi met and vowed to fight on.

May 11, 1865, Confederate President Jefferson Davis was captured by Union forces. It is believed he was attempting to reach the Department of the Trans-Mississippi.

It wasn't until May 26, 1865 that the Department of the Trans-Mississippi surrendered at New Orleans, officially ending the Civil War in the west.

For many, however, those from Missouri who fought on the Confederate side in particular, the war continued.

Sultana: A Case For Sabotage

Murderer of the Age

"...the result of no accident, but of fiendish design, and locates with much particularity the boss dynamiter and murderer of the age."[1]

Seven miles out of Memphis, at 2 a. m. on April 27, 1865, the steamer *Sultana* chugged northward loaded with over twenty-three hundred people, most of them Union soldiers returning home from southern prison camps. Without warning, an explosion ripped through the boilers. Scalding steam burst out. A shower of flaming coal shot upward into the night, raining downward on the crowded boat.[2] In moments the steamer was engulfed in flames.

Over seventeen hundred people died,[3] making the destruction of the *Sultana* a maritime disaster worse than the sinking of the *Titanic*.

At any other time, the event would have raised an outcry of concern and questions, but it faded quickly into near-obscurity, for less than two weeks earlier President Lincoln had been assassinated. The attention of both nations, Union and Confederate, was focused eastward, first on Lee's surrender in Virginia followed days later by the death of Lin-Lincoln.

---

[1] *St. Louis Globe-Democrat*, May 6, 1888.

[2] Potter, Jerry O. *The Sultana Tragedy: America's Greatest Maritime Disaster*, Pelican Publishing Company, Inc. 1992 (hereafter "Potter").

[3] There is no completely accurate count of deaths, and some dispute about the total. 1700 to 1800 is a fair number, though there were possibly over 1800 deaths.

Three investigations into the *Sultana* disaster followed.[4] Only a brief time was spent in Memphis seeking the exact cause of the explosion before moving to concentrate on who was responsible for so overloading the boat in Vicksburg. Though sabotage was not conclusively ruled out, neither was it strongly investigated. The destruction of the *Sultana* was eventually dismissed as the result of either a flaw in the boilers, a faulty boiler repair, or negligence in letting the water level fall too low in the boilers.

Sultana on the last voyage - Library of Congress

There the matter remained until twenty-three years after the disaster. On May 6, 1888 an article appeared in the *St. Louis Globe-Democrat* saying a St. Louis, Missouri resident named William C. Streetor claimed a "Confederate mail carrier and blockade runner" named "Robert Lowden," alias "Charles Dale," had actually destroyed the *Sultana* in an act of sabotage. "...for I had the statement from his own lips," Streetor told the newspaper.

---

4 National Archives and Records Administration—Record Group 153, unnumbered microfilm series, Washburn Commission Records, Dana Commission Records, Hoffman Investigation Records

The *Memphis Daily Appeal* printed a substantially abbreviated version of the article on May 8, 1888[5] but it had little effect, with most historians dismissing it as a mere footnote in history. James W. Elliot in *Transport to Disaster* said of the suggestion of sabotage that "the idea was adopted by the usual weird assortment of cranks and publicity seekers."[6] He then mentions the article with the Streetor claim.

Streetor was neither a crank nor a publicity seeker. Nor was he alone in believing the *Sultana* was destroyed by sabotage. Far from it. Looking at the scanty Memphis article, though, it was easy for later researchers to dismiss the claim of the unknown man.

The answers to the fate of the *Sultana* were not to be found in Memphis, where the tragedy occurred, nor in Vicksburg, where the original Federal investigations focused, but in St. Louis, Missouri. In St. Louis, were to be found two extremely significant things: The identities, and histories, of *Streetor* and *Lowden*.

---

[5] Most *Sultana* historians to date have cited the *Memphis Daily Appeal* article, as the search for information about the disaster has, naturally, centered around Memphis. In the Memphis article, Streetor's name is misspelled "Streeter."

[6] Elliot, James W. *Transport to Disaster*, Holt, Rinehart and Winston 1962 (hereafter "Elliot")

William C. Streetor

The St. Louis resident who made the claim of Confederate sabotage against the *Sultana* was William Crandall Streetor, a sign painter in St. Louis. Streetor had enlisted in the Union Army in St. Louis early in 1861.[7] Streetor was also the assistant keeper and chief clerk of Gratiot Street Prison, the Federal prison established in St. Louis in December 1861, working for the Provost Marshal's office.[8]

Born in Auburn, New York, April 20, 1838, William C. Streetor was the grandson of American Revolutionary War soldier Zebina Day, one of the Green Mountain Boys, who served throughout the war for independence.[9]

Like many in the early, tangled days of the Civil War in St. Louis, Streetor was at Camp Jackson as a member of the Missouri state militia when Union commander Nathaniel Lyon arrested the entire camp as presumed rebels—as were Robert Louden and his brother-in-law Arthur McCoy—but immediately thereafter Streetor firmly chose the Union side. A musician as well as a painter, Streetor enlisted as his unit's Drum Major,[10] as had his Revolutionary War grandfather.

---

[7] National Archives and Records Administration (hereafter NARA), Records Group (RG) 94, M405, roll 402, Compiled Service Records, 3rd US Res. Corp.

[8] NARA, RG 109, M416, rolls 90, 91, 92, Union Provost Marshal's Files of Papers Relating to Two or More Civilians, rolls 90-92 regard Gratiot St. Prison / payroll records in George E. Leighton collection at Missouri Historical Society

[9] Sons of the American Revolution Membership Applications, 1889-1970. Louisville, Kentucky: National Society of the Sons of the American Revolution, Volume: 20; SAR Membership Number: 3837.

[10] The Missouri Historical Society has Streetor's drum in their collections, donated by his daughter.

Streetor enlisted in the U.S. 3rd Missouri Res. on May 13th or 14th of 1861.[11]

Later, as a respected member of the Union army veteran fraternal organization Grand Army of the Republic, his comrades said of Streetor, "In his military life he discharged every duty assigned him in a thorough and satisfactory manner. Afterward, in every-day life, as told by those with whom he was associated, he discharged his duties in the line of business with credit to himself and to the satisfaction of those with whom he was joined in interest."[12] A business profile praised his "...well-merited reputation for excellent work, promptness and reliability."[13]

William C. Streetor married early in the war years, and had a son and daughter born to him and his wife, Lucinda, in 1862 and 1864.

On December, 22, 1861, when the first Confederate prisoners arrived in St. Louis at what soon came to be called Gratiot Street Prison the temporary keeper there to admit them was William C. Streetor. Throughout the war he served primarily as chief clerk and assistant keeper of the prison. The handwriting in the prison registers documenting prisoner arrivals—including Robert Louden's—is William C. Streetor's.

---

[11] NARA, RG 94, M405, roll 402. All Streetor's enlistment records in NARA and with the U.S. government give his enlistment date as May 8, 1861, which is at odds with his having been at Camp Jackson on May 10th. Forms used at the time of his enlistment had the date pre-filled in with the date the unit was mustered into service, rather than each individual's actual date of enlistment. Streetor's honorable service was researched and confirmed by both the U.S. Bureau of Pensions, and by the Grand Army of the Republic.

[12] Grand Army of the Republic, read in Ransom Post December 5, 1920, "In Memoriam," Missouri Historical Society.

[13] *Pen and Sunlight Sketches of St. Louis*, Phoenix Publishing Company, Chicago, Illinois, 1898.

Streetor also, after the war, worked in a painting business with Robert Louden.[14] If anyone was in a position to know Louden's secrets, it was Streetor.

Gratiot Street Prison

[14] Grimes, Absalom C. *Confederate Mail Runner*, edited by M. M. Quaife, Yale University Press, 1926 (hereafter "Grimes") / *St. Louis Globe-Democrat*, May 6, 1888 / supporting source *St. Louis Business Directory*, 1867.

Robert Louden

The man Streetor claimed told him he blew up the *Sultana* was Robert Louden (note spelling), a Confederate agent who was not only a mail smuggler and spy, but was notorious for the destruction of steamboats along the Mississippi River.

"...there is not another man in this or any other state as dangerous a spy as this R. Louden," said St. Louis Provost Marshal George E. Leighton in 1863.[15]

Robert Louden was the eldest son of Scottish immigrants Andrew Louden, a carpenter, and his wife Christina.[16] Robert was a native of Philadelphia, Pennsylvania where, as a young man, he worked as a painter.[17]

On October 26, 1851, in Philadelphia, Robert Louden and a friend, James McFadden, got into a fight and killed a man named Henry McGeary. "...rival gangs of rowdies," some newspapers said of the violent street fight, "assassination" and "brutal murder," others called it. The victim was slashed and stabbed, his face cut apart, and his neck slashed. A stab to the ribs killed McGeary. The killing apparently took place as part of the violence between competing fire companies.[18]

---

[15] NARA, RG 109, M345, roll 170, Union Provost Marshal's Files of Papers Relating to Individual Civilians

[16] Her name is listed as Cecelia in the 1850 census but as Christina or Christine in all following censuses, marriage information, Philadelphia directories, and death certificate.

[17] 1850 US Census, Pennsylvania, Philadelphia County, Spruce Ward, page 347

[18] *New York Daily Times* October 28, 1851, October 30, 1851, November 7, 1851, November 27, 1852, November 29, 1852; testimony of Andrew Close October 1864; Pennsylvania, Philadelphia City Death Certificates, 1803–1915;

Louden's friend, McFadden, was arrested immediately, but Louden got away. He was vigorously sought in cities across the east, but fled to St. Louis, Missouri.

Robert Louden arrived in St. Louis using the name Charlie Deal. Not long after arriving, he was drawn to the St. Louis fire companies, as he had been in Philadelphia. A vengeful member of a rival fire company discovered Louden's secret and turned him in to the authorities.[19] Robert Louden, a.k.a. Charlie Deal, was arrested and taken back to Philadelphia where in late November of 1852 he stood trial for murder. Louden was, instead, convicted of manslaughter on November 27, 1852, and sentenced to three years and eight months in prison. He was sent to Eastern State Penitentiary on December 3, 1852 to serve his sentence. At the time it was noted he was "temperate." Robert Louden was nineteen-years-old.[20]

Eastern State Prison

Prisoners at Eastern State Penitentiary were totally isolated from all human contact on the theory that they would reflect on their crimes and become penitent. Instead the solitary confinement and complete silence of the prison became known as a "maniac maker," with a disproportionately high rate of insanity among the prisoners. Some

---

[19] Testimony of Andrew Close, October 1864, NARA, RG 109, M345, roll 170.

[20] Pennsylvania State Archives, Eastern State Penitentiary Administration Records, RG 15, Descriptive Registers 6-3946, Admission and Discharge Registers 6-1814 / NARA RG 94, M797, roll 40, Case File Investigations by Levi C. Turner and Lafayette C. Baker 1861-1866, report 1226 on Robert Louden by Chief of Police of Philadelphia, Benjamin Franklin.

prisoners were pardoned as their mental conditions deteriorated. Charles Dickens, in *American Notes*, said of Eastern State, "It is my fixed opinion that those who have undergone this punishment MUST pass into society again morally unhealthy and diseased... What monstrous phantoms, bred of despondency and doubt, and born and reared in solitude, have stalked upon the earth, making creation ugly, and darkening the face of Heaven!"[21]

Robert Louden was released with a pardon May 19, 1854 with over a year remaining on his original sentence. Prison records do not reveal the reason he was pardoned. Louden left Philadelphia, returning to St. Louis again using the name "Charles Deal."

As Charles Deal, Louden was a member of the Liberty Fire Company No. 6. The Liberty Fire Company was one of the combative, competitive volunteer fire companies in 1850's St. Louis. Thomas Lynch, writing a history of the volunteer fire companies, said of the Liberty, "they acquired

Liberty Fire Company

unfortunately more of the Eastern rowdies than all the rest [of the fire companies] combined." The volunteer fire companies were abolished in 1858 in favor of professional organizations. The Liberty Fire House was burned February 11, 1858 by, Lynch says, "some of the disaffected members."[22]

Before its demise, the volunteer fire department gave Louden valuable social, political, and business connections in the city. One prominent member of Liberty was John M. Wimer, mayor of St. Louis. In 1860 Wimer's business partner was a man named Thomas E. Courtenay, a businessman

[21] Dickens, Charles, *American Notes for General Circulation*, 1842

[22] Lynch, Thomas, *Volunteer Fire Department of St. Louis*, 1880, from Missouri Historical Society

who was also sheriff of St. Louis County at that time.[23] Courtenay would later play a key role in Louden's sabotage of the *Sultana.*

On August 31, 1858, using his correct name, Louden married Mary Jeanette Gibson. She was the sister of Louisa Gibson McCoy, wife of Arthur C. McCoy[24], another member of the Liberty Fire Company. McCoy became a Confederate captain, scout, and spy under General Jo. Shelby. Later McCoy became notorious as one of the "Terrible Quintette," the original gang of bank robbers ultimately known to history as the James-Younger Gang.

One of Robert Louden's younger brothers, James, who worked as a bricklayer, joined him in St. Louis. James was also a member of the Liberty Fire Company, using the name "James Deal" on the roster.[25]

Louden's new wife, Mary Gibson, was a young widow with two children by her late first husband, William L. Lynch (brother of later fire company historian Thomas Lynch).

---

[23] John M. Wimer was mayor in 1860. He died in battle in 1863 as a Confederate Colonel. Wimer and Courtenay were real estate and general agents in business together (Edwards 1860 *St. Louis City Directory*).

[24] Arthur C. McCoy was one of founders of the "Minute Men" who, with Basil Duke, Colton Greene, J. Rock Champion, and James Quinlan, raised a Missouri state flag over the St. Louis Courthouse in March 1861. The secessionist flag they flew over the Minute Men headquarters was said to have been sewn by Louisa Gibson McCoy. (*Reminiscences of Basil Duke* by General Basil Duke, 1911). After the war McCoy was alleged to have been involved in several bank and train robberies with the James-Younger gang. In St. Louis newspapers at the time, the outlaw band was known as the Arthur McCoy Gang. Later, some of Arthur's children, in family histories, remembered being admitted for free to a certain St. Louis theater, where the doorman at the time was Frank James. In "A Terrible Quintette," a lengthy article published by John Newman Edwards, author of *Noted Guerrillas* and adjutant to General Shelby, names as the "terrible quintette" Arthur C. McCoy, Cole and John Younger, and Frank and Jesse James.

[25] Lynch, Thomas, *Volunteer Fire Departments of St. Louis*, 1880, from Missouri Historical Society.

When Robert Louden wed Mary Gibson he married into one of the oldest families in Missouri. His mother-in-law was Heloise Daguet Gibson, who descended from some of the earliest French settlers in Ste. Genevieve, Missouri. Louden's father-in-law, William Gibson, was closely related to the Dent family—the in-laws of Ulysses S. Grant. Soon after his marriage into this well-to-do family, Louden went into business for himself, painting houses, signs, and—significantly—steamboats.[26]

Robert and Mary Louden's marriage was to be a strange and turbulent thing, however, filled with long spans when they were apart. In 1860 her first husband's estate was finally settled, yielding Mary little. At this time she listed herself as a widow in the St. Louis City Directory—not the last time she would do that while husband Robert Louden still lived—and in the census is shown living separately from him. They were separated when daughter Mollie Louden was born June 2, 1860. Whether the cause of their separation was marital strife, financial troubles, or to simplify the final resolution of William Lynch's estate settlement (in the paperwork in 1860 she signed herself as Mary J. Lynch), Mary and Robert Louden reunited as the swirling maelstrom of history again drew close around them.

St. Louis in early 1861 was a city divided in loyalties. The divisions in the city were not easily defined as they varied from house to house, and within families. Though an eastern northerner by upbringing, Robert Louden chose the southern cause, joining the Minute Men in St. Louis. A report on their activities claimed that Robert Louden and Arthur McCoy were dangerous men and "the head and front of all mischief." The man making the report said that Louden and McCoy had a plan to kill leading Missouri unionist Frank Blair.[27] The spy regarded the threat as serious.

---

[26] 1859 *St. Louis City Directory*

[27] NARA RG 109, M345, roll 170, letter by George E. Leighton / Broadhead Papers, 1861 spy report to the Union Safety Committee, Missouri Historical Society

Two of Robert Louden's brothers, James and Andrew, also went with the Confederacy,[28] while their sister's husband joined the Union army.[29]

Robert Louden again came to Union officials' attention on June 30th of 1862 when he was charged with "giving expression to treasonable sentiments."[30] No action was taken on the charge. Little did the officials know that Louden was already an active Confederate courier and mail carrier. It's possible he was already responsible for the burning of Mississippi River steamboats.[31] Charles Parsons, of the Union Quartermasters department, listed the first steamboat destroyed in St. Louis by "incendiary fire" during the war taking place in October of 1861.[32]

St. Louis levee before the war

---

[28] NARA, RG 109, M345, roll 170, letter by George E. Leighton / NARA RG 109, M269 roll 244, service records of Andrew Louden.

[29] Pvt. David A. Thompson, New York, enlisted May 13, 1861 C Co. 79th Inf Reg. NY discharged with disability at Annapolis, Maryland on February 22, 1863, *married to Elizabeth Louden.*

[30] NARA, RG 109, M345, roll 170.

[31] Grimes suggests that at this time Louden was already active as a boat-burner. There were suspicious boat-burnings for which Louden cannot be ruled out as a suspect by time and location.

[32] Charles Parsons Papers, ledger of steamboats destroyed, Missouri Historical Society.

Absalom C. Grimes

Earlier in June of 1862, Robert Louden met the "Official Confederate Mail Carrier" for General Sterling Price's army, Absalom C. Grimes. Before the war Grimes had been a

steamboat pilot on the upper Mississippi River. He had been relatively neutral until John B. Gray[33] tried to force Grimes and several other steamer pilots (including Sam Bowen and Samuel Clemens—later better known as Mark Twain) into service ferrying troops on the Missouri River.[34] Grimes then joined the southern cause with enthusiasm, causing a breach in his own family as a younger brother joined the Union army.[35] After a stint as a private in

Absalom C. Grimes
about 1863

the cavalry, during which he was captured and escaped twice, Grimes decided to carry letters from Missouri families with him as he went south to rejoin his unit. The letters were so gratefully received that Grimes was commissioned as a

---

[33] Brigadier-General John B. Gray, Adjutant-General of the State of Missouri, originally Colonel John B. Gray, 1st Infantry Missouri State Militia.

[34] Grimes.

[35] NARA, RG 109, M322 roll 4, Compiled Service Records, 1st Mo. Cav. CSA, letter by Mrs. Charlotte Grimes to Provost Marshal requesting permission to visit her son / Enlistment records Charles F. Grimes, Co. H, 142nd Inf. Reg. IL/Co. I, 149th Inf. Reg. IL

major on detached secret service duty,[36] assigned as an official mail carrier by General Sterling Price.[37]

Records of Louden's official military career are sketchy. He was in the Minute Men, an early pro-Confederate organization[38]. Louden and McCoy had been captured at Camp Jackson and exchanged.[39] An 1863 Federal report says he was a Confederate captain under General Price.[40] Grimes' daughter, in a post-war magazine article, claims Louden had been a major.[41]

Robert Louden and Absalom Grimes became partners in the mail carrying and courier business, both of them passing through the lines numerous times, moving about freely within Union territory, with Memphis one of their main hubs. While carrying mail between families and lonely soldiers may seem a harmless enough enterprise, the Union had early on declared mail carrying to be the equivalent of spying and punishable by death. Captured Rebel mail was a tremendous prize for the wealth of information about troop strengths and movements the letters contained, as well as identifying Confederate-sympathizing citizens. Waves of arrests in St. Louis followed closely after the capture of any

---

[36] NARA, RG 109, M322 roll 4, Compiled Service Records, 1st Mo. Cav. CSA, service records of Absalom C. Grimes.

[37] Grimes. In Federal records he's often referred to as "The Rebel Mail Carrier."

[38] Union Provost Marshal George E. Leighton describes Louden as a "strong Minute Man" (NARA RG 109, M345, roll 170). A "Louden" appears on a roster of Company D, McLaren Guards (Hopewell, M. M. C., *Camp Jackson: History of the Missouri Volunteer Militia of St. Louis*, 1861, Two Trails Publishing, 1997).

[39] M. E. F. Pollock Papers, Record of Camp Jackson Parolees Exchanged for Federal Prisoners After the Battle of Lexington, Missouri Historical Society.

[40] NARA, RG 94, M797 roll 40.

[41] "The Blockade Runners of Vicksburg" by Mrs. Charlotte Grimes Mitchell, *Valley Trust Magazine*, Volume 6, Number 1, July, 1928.

Rebel mail.[42] Coupled with this, both Louden and Grimes carried official Confederate dispatches to other agents who worked behind the lines, and to secret Rebel organizations. Louden seems to have been one of the primary couriers between General Price and northern Copperhead organizations.[43]

Grimes, in his memoirs, praised Louden's "unlimited courage and good judgment" in their dangerous work. He also referred to Louden, "amusing himself burning government steamboats."[44] Louden's experience as a fireman certainly gave him the knowledge of how to effectively make things burn. His business painting steamboats also taught him both their operations, and their vulnerabilities. With a partner in Ab Grimes, who knew almost everyone on every steamboat on the Mississippi River, they were set to be a very effective team.

---

[42] *Official Records Of The Union And Confederate Navies In The War Of The Rebellion* (hereafter Navy OR), Series 1 Volume 24, page 427, Report of Acting Lieutenant Woodworth, U. S. Navy, regarding the delivery of intercepted mail captured on steamer *White Cloud. The patterns of arrests following captured mails in St. Louis can also be seen in the Gratiot Street Prison ledgers, NARA RG 109, M598, roll 72 and Provost Marshal files NARA RG 109, M416, rolls 90-92 as well as blunt statements in St. Louis newspapers saying stories of captured mail had been withheld until arrests had been made.*

[43] Louden's recorded movements and locations in northern cities such as Chicago, Detroit, and Indianapolis, plus the content of his captured mails, supports this claim: NARA RG 109, M345, roll 170, 171 / RG 94, M797, roll 40 / Grimes.

[44] Grimes.

Spies and Mail Carriers

According to Grimes, by July of 1862 Federal authorities had become aware of the existence of a regular mail service between the Rebels in Missouri and the Confederate army. Peter Tallon—later Chief of U.S. Police in St. Louis—described a July 1862 encounter with Louden. The two went from saloon to saloon together while Louden delivered letters from the southern army. Tallon became Chief of U.S. Police the following year.[45] On August 11, 1862 Louden was arrested in a St. Louis saloon with about one hundred letters in his possession.[46]

Louden was taken to Gratiot Street Prison, the main Union prison in St. Louis. There to receive him was the assistant keeper of the prison, William C. Streetor.[47]

Charged with mail carrying, and being in the Rebel army and within Union lines without permission, Louden was sentenced to imprisonment for the duration of the war. He was transferred to Alton Prison twenty-five miles away, across the Mississippi River, in Illinois on August 20th, but Louden jumped overboard from the boat carrying him there, and escaped.[48]

Soon after, on September 2, 1862, Grimes was arrested in St. Louis with a large south-bound mail. He was tried on charges of being a mail carrier and spy and sentenced to be

---

[45] NARA, RG 109, M345, roll 170, report of Capt. Peter Tallon dated October 1863 referring to incidents of July 1862.

[46] NARA, RG 109, M345, roll 170.

[47] George E. Leighton Papers, Provost Marshal payroll records, Missouri Historical Society.

[48] NARA, RG 109, M345, roll 170 / *St. Louis Democrat*, September 4, 1863.

shot. Though held in close confinement, chained and heavily guarded, Grimes again demonstrated his talent for escaping a month later from Gratiot Street Prison, cutting through the floor, and out through the foundation. When his disappearance was discovered, it was Streetor who found Grimes' means of escape when he "stepped on the end of one of the cut planks and down he went."[49]

Though Louden and Grimes had both received a clear taste of the perils of their professions, they didn't slacken their mail smuggling and courier activities. Grimes said of Louden that "the sideline of steamboat burning was accredited to him and he was, therefore, much in demand by the Federals."[50] A Federal report at the end of November 1862 said that twenty steamers had been destroyed within the previous two months.[51] Some of these were likely the work of Robert Louden. "He told me he had fired no less than half a dozen steamboats on the Mississippi," Streetor later said.[52]

On December 3, 1862, Robert and Mary Louden's baby daughter, Mary J., died in St. Louis and was buried in Calvary Cemetery near their infant son, James A. Louden, who had died in March.[53] Robert Louden, wanted by Federal authorities, probably could not attend his daughter's burial.

---

[49] Grimes.

[50] Ibid.

[51] Navy OR, Series 1 Volume 23 Page 511, letter by Lewis B. Parsons, Colonel and Assistant Quartermaster.

[52] *St. Louis Globe-Democrat*, May 6, 1888.

[53] Calvary Cemetery burial records / St. Louis city death records.

Louden's Family Targeted

Efforts to find Louden reached a new level. On April 25, 1863, Louden's wife Mary was arrested.[54] She was taken to Gratiot Street Prison where she was pressured to reveal her husband's location. An officer of the prison tormented Mary, taunting her about her baby's recent death, once coming to her late at night to tell her (falsely) that her other baby, two-year-old Mollie,[55] had also died. Mary became extremely ill, coughing and choking on her own blood, yet medical care was denied her. The cell in which she was kept had been a room in which dissections had been conducted when the building was a medical college, the floors were stained with old blood. When the floors above were washed, the washwater—foul with urine and tobacco spit—ran down through the ceiling, drenching her.[56]

While Mary was imprisoned in St. Louis, in Philadelphia, on May 3, 1863 Louden's father was arrested and taken to Fort McHenry, Maryland. A Rebel mail had been delivered in Philadelphia and suspicion fell on Andrew Louden. It was soon learned that his son, Robert, was responsible. "The military authorities of St. Louis are very desirous of catching young Loudon as they wish to try him as a spy and hang

---

[54] NARA, RG 109, M598 rolls 72, 145, Gratiot prison ledgers / NARA, RG 109, M345, roll 170.

[55] Mollie Louden (Conroy – Bell), June 2, 1860 – April 22, 1896.

[56] Missouri Division of the United Daughters of the Confederacy *Reminiscences of the Women of Missouri During the Sixties, Reminiscences of Mrs. Lucy Nickolson Lindsay*, reprinted by Morningside House, Inc. 1988 (hereafter "Rem. Women"). *Supporting evidence of the conditions in Gratiot Street Prison at this time are found in Federal inspection reports: War Of The Rebellion: A Compilation of the Official Records of the Union and Confederate Armies* (hereafter OR), Series II—Volume VI, page 150.

him," said a letter by Lt. Col. William Whipple who had ordered the father's arrest.[57] Instead of being released, Andrew Louden was banished to the south, never having been convicted of any crime. His family believed he had been killed.

On May 13, 1863 Robert Louden's wife, along with two dozen other civilian citizens of St. Louis, half of them women, most from Grimes' and Louden's mail smuggling ring, were banished. Mary Louden was forced to leave her young daughters behind. With the others, Mary was put on board a steamer and sent, under guard, down the river to Memphis.

Another of the banished women, Margaret McLure,[58] in later years, recalled the name of the steamer that carried them into exile as the *Sultana*.[59] Several St. Louis newspapers, however, stated that the boat was the *Belle Memphis*.[60] Several factors come together at this point that may have given Robert Louden a very real and personal reason to later specifically target the *Sultana*. The two boats were side-wheelers close to the same size.[61] Records indicate that the *Sultana* would have arrived in Memphis at about the same time as exiles on the *Belle Memphis*.[62] Given the remem-

---

[57] NARA, RG 109, M345, roll 170.

[58] Margaret McClure was banished, in part, for her role in assisting Grimes' mail smuggling organization. She also aided escaped Confederate prisoners. Her home was seized and turned into Chestnut Street Prison, in which numerous St. Louis women were confined, including Grimes' aunt, Marion Wall Vail, and his cousin Lizzie Ivers.

[59] *Rem. Women*, "History of Events Preceding and Following the Banishment of Mrs. Margaret A. McLure, as Given to the Author by Herself."

[60] Winter, William C. *The Civil War in St. Louis: A Guided Tour*, Missouri Historical Society Press 1994, citing *Missouri Republican*, May 14, 1863, and *Missouri Democrat*, May 14, 1863.

[61] *Belle Memphis*: length=263, beam=38, depth=7, 645=tons; *Sultana*: length=260, beam=42, depth=7, 660=tons –Way, Frederick Jr. *Way's Packet Directory*, 1848-1994, Ohio University Press, 1983.

[62] OR, Series I—Volume XXIII/2, page 323.

brance of Margaret McLure, Robert Louden may very well have heard that it was the *Sultana* that carried his sick wife away from her home and children. Another factor in Louden's potential desire for revenge was James Cass Mason. Mason was the captain of the *Belle Memphis* in May of 1863 when Mary Louden was carried into exile.[63] On April 27, 1865, he was the captain of the *Sultana*.

---

[63] Potter.

James Cass Mason and Robert Louden

Mason's and Louden's paths had crossed earlier in 1863 in a curious intersection of events. February 13, 1863, on the river near Memphis, two steamers were stopped, searched and seized by the Federal Gunboat *U.S.S. New Era*. One of these was the steamer *White Cloud*.[64] Found aboard was a large Rebel mail. According to witness testimony, it was Louden's mail, bound south from St. Louis for General Price's army. Louden escaped capture, slipping over the side of the boat and swimming away.

The other steamer seized was the *Rowena* with Rebel contraband found on board.[65] Captain of the *Rowena*, at this time, was J. Cass Mason. The boat was named for Mason's wife, Rowena M. Dozier, and owned by her father, a St. Louis businessman in the river trade. The *Rowena* was confiscated by the Federal government. Apparently because of this event all business relations between Mason and his father-in-law ceased.[66] After this date Mason became captain of the *Belle Memphis* and seems to have halted any smuggling work for the Confederates.

---

[64] NARA RG109, M345, roll 171.

[65] Navy OR, Series I—Volume 24, pages 358, 425-427.

[66] Salecker, Gene Eric, *Disaster on the Mississippi*, (hereafter "Salecker") Naval Institute Press, 1996.

The Boatburners

Through 1863, Robert Louden continued his work with a passion. He and Grimes went through the blockade of Vicksburg—Louden more than once—delivering mail, and carrying messages. After the surrender of Vicksburg, Louden joined Grimes on the Confederate steamer *Prince of Wales*. Along with several other Confederate boats, the *Prince of Wales* was burned to keep it from falling into Union hands. On July 14, 1863 Grimes, probably accompanied by Louden, joined Commander Isaac N. Brown of the Confederate Navy in placing torpedoes that destroyed the Union gunboat *De Kalb*.[67]

During this time in 1863 the boatburners came to be known to the Federals as the "organized boatburners." Though there appears to have been an organization earlier, at this time the boatburners began soliciting the Confederate government for financial support in the form of payment based on the value of Federal property destroyed. Joseph W. Tucker was the leader of the organized boatburners under General Price and his adjutant Colonel Thomas L. Snead. Tucker had been a newspaper editor, and Southern Methodist minister,[68] in St. Louis until he fled south, first to Mississippi, then to Mobile, Alabama. Tucker was part of Sterling Price's political inner circle, editing a newspaper

---

[67] Navy OR, Series I—Volume 25, page 283-286, 290.

[68] "Missouri in Crisis: The Journal of Capt. Albert Tracy," 1861, edited by Ray W. Irwin, *Missouri Historical Review*, Volume LI, January 1957, Number Two (citing Organ, Minnie, "History of the County Press of Missouri," *Missouri Historical Review*, IV, July 1910). Galusha Anderson in *Story of a Border City During the War* (pub. 1908)," says Tucker was a Presbyterian minister.

throughout the war "universally regarded as an 'organ' of Gen. Price."[69]

During the siege of Vicksburg, Tucker solicited $20,000 from Confederate General Joseph E. Johnston to support the boatburning effort.[70] He continued to lobby Richmond for financial support of the boatburners for the rest of the war.[71] The destruction of the steamer *Champion* near Memphis was credited to William Murphy who "received $3000 for doing so from Tucker, this he admits."[72] Other members of the organized boatburners included John Richard Barret, former Missouri congressman from St. Louis, believed by the Federals to have been head of land operations; Thomas L. Clark, a saloon keeper from Grenada, Mississippi[73]; Minor Majors, second in charge under Tucker; and Robert Louden.

---

[69] Reynolds, Thomas C. (Confederate governor-in-exile of Missouri) *General Sterling Price and the Confederacy*, unpublished manuscript, Missouri Historical Society.

[70] OR, Series I—Volume XXIV/3, page 1066.

[71] Tidwell, William A., with James O. Hall and David Winfred Gaddy, *Come Retribution*, Barnes & Noble Books, 1988 / OR, Series IV—Volume III, page- 125, 239 / Letter from Tucker to Jefferson Davis, Jeff. Davis "Constitutionalist."

[72] Charles Parsons Papers, Missouri Historical Society.

[73] Not coincidentally one of Louden and Grimes' mail carrying hubs.

The Steamer *Ruth*

The destruction of the steamer *Ruth* can without doubt be credited to Robert Louden's sabotage. On the night of August 4, 1863, shortly before midnight, after a refueling stop at Cairo, Illinois, the *Ruth* burned.[74] The *Ruth* was en route to Vicksburg with eight Union payroll masters and $2.6 million dollars in army payroll on board. Though heavily

Burning of the Steamer *Ruth*

guarded, the boat and the money were destroyed.[75] Twenty-six of the one hundred fifty passengers, military and civilian, were killed. Grimes, in his memoirs, places the blame squarely on Robert Louden. "At this late date," Grimes finally admitted while writing his memoirs in 1910-1911, "it is safe to say that the account the Federals had against Bob was just and payable."[76] St. Louis Provost Marshal documents also link Louden to the burning of the *Ruth*. Louden

---

[74] Horstman, Ronald, "The Loss of the Government Greenbacks on the Steamer *Ruth*," *Missouri Historical Review*, Volume 70, No. 2, January 1972.

[75] OR, Series I—Volume XXIV/3, page 580 / Series III—Volume III, page 985.

[76] Grimes.

ultimately confessed to destroying the *Ruth*, was tried for the sabotage, and convicted.[77]

On September 3, 1863 Louden's boatburning career was interrupted when he was arrested in St. Louis. The St. Louis newspapers reported on Louden's arrest in gleeful detail. The house in which he was sleeping was surrounded by a squad of cavalry while four U. S. Police officers went in and secured Louden. They wisely declined to accept his word of honor not to escape if they didn't handcuff him, the last wise thing they did that evening. En route to the prison, Louden managed to talk the four police officers into stopping at a saloon for a drink. After downing his liquor, Louden bolted for the door. He was caught hiding in a coal bin and taken to Myrtle Street Prison where, amidst a great deal of "splenetic abuse" aimed at his captors, Louden promised that when he escaped he would "patch his pants with the scalps of Federal soldiers." Louden was "substantially licked" in the one-sided fight that followed.[78]

In Louden's possession at the time of his arrest was a note, in his own hand, dated September 2, 1863 saying, "...I believe we will make a great stroke to-night... everything depends on speed & courage we will have a glorious success or a glorious death."[79] The note is signed with the initials "R. L." with the added initials OAK nearby. OAK was the Order of American Knights, a secret organization trying to conduct the war within Union lines. Though the Order claimed huge numbers of members, and promised grand actions, relatively few key individuals played any real role. In St. Louis, OAK was connected to the organized boatburners who, in turn were connected to, and part of, the Confederate secret ser-

---

[77] NARA, RG 109, M345, roll 170, report to President Lincoln of the case against Robert Louden.

[78] *Missouri Republican* and *St. Louis Democrat*, September 4, 1863.

[79] NARA, RG 109, M345, roll 170.

vice operations.[80] The military head of OAK was General Sterling Price, Louden's commander.

Even though Robert Louden was arrested on the third of September, on the thirteenth his comrades carried out his "great stroke," burning the *Imperial, Jesse K. Bell, Hiawatha, Post Boy*, and a barge loaded with freight at the foot of Market Street in St. Louis. The dollar value of such an event would have been about a quarter of a million 1864 dollars[81] (approximately $4.5 million now). Such incidents were major losses. The organized boat-burners would report on their strikes to Richmond through Tucker, after which payment would be dispensed.

Louden was held for three weeks in Myrtle Street Prison[82] in St. Louis, then moved to Gratiot Street Prison, where he was put in the same cell in which his wife had been kept. A ball and chain were attached to his leg and he was held in close confinement, allowed contact with no one. In a strange letter to his brother Andrew (2nd Lt. Andrew Louden, 16th Mississippi, wounded and captured at Gettysburg, and a POW at Johnson's Island, Ohio)[83] dated November 1, 1863, Robert says he was in St. Louis only to take his daughters to

---

[80] General Sterling Price was military head of the OAK (Castel, Albert, *General Sterling Price and the Civil War in the West,* Louisiana State University Press, 1968 / OR, Series I—Volume VII, page 231, 232 et. al.). Price also authorized the boatburners under Tucker, and a secret service corps under Thomas Courtenay, (OR, Series I—Volume XXII/2, page 970 / OR, Series IV—Volume III, page 202 / Series II—Volume VIII, page 516). There are numerous other sources documenting the connections.

[81] *Encyclopedia of the History of St. Louis* edited by William Hyde and Howard L. Conard, The Southern History Company 1899.

[82] Myrtle Street Prison was a small prison that was administratively part of Gratiot Street Prison.

[83] NARA, RG 109 , M269, roll 244, Compiled Service Records of Confederate Soldiers Who Served in Organizations from the State of Mississippi, 16th Mississippi Inf. Co. A., CSA.

a Convent.[84] He talks about Mary, her banishment and how he hadn't seen her but once.[85] Then he writes about the cruel and inhuman way the Federals treated his father, and that his mother, "was about frantic at his loss and the way they murdered him." He then writes about taking revenge, saying his brother-in-law, Arthur McCoy, had "a double duty to perform now, fight for freedom & revenge both."[86] The letter is strange in that it seems aimed directly at the Provost Marshal officials who would read it first, rather than at his brother, whose own reply sounded rather puzzled. Louden's father returned to Philadelphia from the south four days after this letter was written,[87] so Louden probably didn't know he was still alive. The tone of this letter is dark and bitter.

Louden was tried in December on charges of being a mail carrier, spy, and boatburner, having burned the steamer *Ruth*. He was found guilty on all charges and sentenced to be hanged.[88] Louden's mail-running partner, Absalom Grimes, was arrested in Memphis in November and returned to St. Louis where he was also tried and sentenced to death.[89]

---

[84] When Louden was arrested he said he had come to St. Louis to turn himself in.

[85] They made good use of the brief time they had together near Memphis when Mary was sent into exile—Mary had another baby precisely nine months later.

[86] NARA, RG 109, M345, roll 170.

[87] NARA, RG 94, M797, roll 40, Levi C. Turner case files—the elder Louden was reported by Federal agents to have left Richmond, made his way to Fortress Monroe, escaped from there by unknown means, returning to his home in Philadelphia November 5, 1863, where his arrival was immediately reported by agents.

[88] NARA, RG 109, M345, roll 170.

[89] Grimes was not charged with being a boatburner. He was convicted of being a spy and mail carrier.

Under Sentence of Death

As the date of his execution neared, Louden wrote a letter pleading for clemency. He confessed his guilt to all charges, including boatburning, saying, "...I am deeply and truly penitent for all I have done and pray for forgiveness." After talking about the plight of his "afflicted wife and helpless family" he ends by "solemnly pledging never again to transgress the laws of my country."[90] In considering his promise, it would be well to remember that to Robert Louden "my country" was the C.S.A., not the U.S.A. Streetor later called Louden, "cool and calculating in his disposition."[91]

A last-minute reprieve arrived May 6, 1864, only hours before Louden was to be hanged. Grimes says it was due to the intervention of a St. Louis priest and nun. However, Louden's mother had rushed to Washington, D. C. to plead with the President for clemency when she learned of her son's impending execution. A telegram dated May 5th from the President's office enquiring if the execution date had been set suggests her interview with Lincoln may have saved her son's life. The reprieve from President Lincoln cited the Union connections and loyalty of the rest of Robert Louden's family.[92]

But it was only a reprieve. The death sentence hung over Louden during the summer of 1864 as the St. Louis Order of American Knights leaders, Dunn, Hunt, and others, were arrested and confessed the secrets of their organization.[93]

---

[90] NARA, RG 109, M345, roll 170.

[91] St. Louis Globe-Democrat, May 6, 1888.

[92] NARA, RG 109, M345, roll 170.

[93] OR—Sanderson Report: statement of Charles L. Hunt, Series II—Volume VII, pages 317-321, statement of Charles E. Dunn, pages 628-641.

In June of 1864, with his own execution date nearing, Grimes led a desperate escape attempt in which several men were killed. Grimes was shot and it was thought for a time that he would die. Louden was involved in the escape attempt but didn't succeed.[94] Several others did get away. Among them were Jasper C. Hill and William H. Sebring, both of whom made their way to Canada where they joined Thomas H. Hines, Bennett H. Young, John B. Castleman, and others recommended by C. L. Vallandigham, in the failed Confederate secret service/Order of American Knights scheme to free the prisoners of war at Camp Douglas in Chicago.[95]

On October 3, 1864, with the Federals believing General Price's invasion from Arkansas was threatening the security of the St. Louis prisons, Louden, and a number of other prisoners from Gratiot, were transferred to Alton Prison a short distance up the river in Illinois. Grimes, in the prison hospital, still recovering from his earlier escape attempt, managed to smuggle a file to Louden.[96] While on the steam-

---

[94] Grimes.

[95] Headley, John W. *Confederate Operations in Canada and New York*, chapter XXIII, The Neale Publishing Company, 1906 / Report of Committee of R. E. Lee Camp No. 58 U. C. V. Appointed to Investigate Charges Against Gen. Wm. H. Sebring, 1915—Florida State Archives. *This latter document contains letters and statements from Young and Castleman regarding this incident, also a copy of instructions Confederate Torpedo Bureau head, Gabriel Rains, had given to William H. Sebring on the construction of an incendiary cartridge. Sebring adds the note that Rains was "Chief of the Secret Service of the Confederate Government, and my orders were direct from him." While in Gratiot Street Prison with Grimes, Sebring began a mail correspondence with one of Grimes' and Louden's main smuggling associates in Memphis, Miss Annie Perdue. She had been sought immediately after Louden's arrest because of mail involving her found in his possession (NARA, RG 109, M345, rolls 170, 270). When Grimes was arrested in Memphis he says Annie Perdue was also brought in as the Federals suspected their association. In 1866 Sebring and Perdue married.*

[96] Grimes.

er to Alton, Louden filed through the chain that handcuffed him to another prisoner, slipped over the side of the boat, and escaped.

Advisories were widely circulated with Louden's description. Everyone who may have had any connection to Louden's escape, *except* Grimes, was questioned vigorously,[97] but he was not found.

Louden's wife, who had been allowed to return to the north after his arrest, had gone with the children to Philadelphia to stay with his family. A telegram was sent from St. Louis to Philadelphia instructing authorities there to arrest Mary Louden and Robert's father Andrew, and to hold them as hostages in case Louden attempted to go there.[98]

Louden and Lynch family gravesites in St. Louis,
only the grave of Louden's daughter, Mollie, still has a marker.
Buried here are Mary Gibson Louden, her mother Heloise Gibson,
two infant children, daughter Mollie, & 1st husband William Lynch

---

[97] NARA, RG 109, M345, roll 170.

[98] NARA, RG 109, M345, roll 170.

Hunted

Robert Louden
5 ft 8 or 9 in high
30 or 35 years old
Light-Complexion dark hair very
remarkable large blue eyes with a great
deal of white in them, constantly rolling
never resting long on one object—
Weighs from 160 to 170 lbs
Of good address, uses a great deal
of profane language, would be
called a smart active fellow

Louden description - NARA

For several months there was no word of Robert Louden. Grimes said Louden had successfully made his escape to the south. Streetor confirms, he "made his way South, where he remained until after the close of the war."[99]

James H. Baker, Provost Marshal General of the Department of the Missouri, continued to investigate the boatburners. William Murphy of New Orleans turned himself in, named his comrades, then vanished.[100] In February, Baker arrested, among several others, Edward Frazor, a steamboat striker from St. Louis, who made a full confession naming the other boatburners and described their connec-

---

[99] *St. Louis Globe-Democrat*, May 6, 1888.

[100] OR, Series I—Volume XLVIII/2, pages 194-196.

tion to the Confederate government.[101] Robert Louden's name was prominent on a list headed by Tucker, Majors, and Barret.[102]

The hunt for Louden intensified in March of 1865. Advisories were sent out from St. Louis to a number of cities with his description and orders to arrest him. Louden was thought to have been arrested in New Orleans. Though authorities there claimed Louden had never been in their custody Baker still believed Louden had gone to New Orleans. The city was searched thoroughly. Several of the officers in New Orleans knew Louden and had a photograph of him.[103]

At this same time Louden's former smuggling partner, Absalom Grimes, made a trip to New Orleans. Grimes had been granted a pardon from President Lincoln on December 10, 1864[104] due to the influence of several of his Union steamboat colleagues and friends. Grimes married his fiancée, Lucy Glascock of Ralls County, Missouri, March 7, 1865 and a short time thereafter took a honeymoon trip to New Orleans on the steamer *Henry Von Phul*. The pilot of the *Von Phul* was Sam Bowen, a friend of Grimes who had aided the smuggling efforts throughout the war.[105]

The oddness of Grimes choosing to go to New Orleans at this time is striking. Grimes was a known Confederate agent who had been actively sought up and down the river. Two weeks after being pardoned he was arrested by the sheriff in Hannibal, Missouri, a place Grimes was well-known, who hadn't heard of his release. He also had a close call with some Federal soldiers seeking to lynch him.[106] The Missis-

---

[101] NARA, RG 109, M345, roll 97, Baker's report on Frazor.

[102] OR, Series I—Volume XLVIII/2, pages 194-196.

[103] NARA, RG 109, M345, roll 170, 171.

[104] NARA, RG 109, M345, roll 112.

[105] Grimes.

[106] Grimes.

sippi River was far from safe and secure. Not only was it still a war zone, but at every Union-held town along the way were Federal officials who probably didn't know of his pardon. Though Grimes' memoirs casually describe the trip as "all sunshine," it was an enormously risky thing for a person in his position to undertake for anything less than an important cause.

If, as Baker believed, Louden was in New Orleans in late March, and being actively sought, Grimes' arrival in a friendly steamer was the perfect opportunity to leave the city and head for a safer area.

Such a safer area would describe Memphis, where Louden had numerous reliable associates. Throughout the war, Memphis had been a major hub in Louden's and Grimes' smuggling work. Not least among those in the area of Memphis at this time was Arthur C. McCoy, Louden's brother-in-law. Commanding a small band of Shelby's men on the Arkansas side set to watch the river and do what damage they could, McCoy was also sending spies into and out of Memphis.[107] Louden could certainly have counted on McCoy for support.

Grimes and his new wife arrived back in St. Louis the day Lincoln died. Though Grimes gives details of Louden's escape in October 1864, his memoirs are extremely quiet about Louden's activities during 1865. With a pardon dated December of 1864, Grimes had good cause to keep quiet about any unpardoned association with Louden during early 1865.

In April of 1865, just days before the *Sultana* arrived in Memphis, letters were going out from the St. Louis Provost Marshal's office naming nineteen men to whom Baker attributed the destruction of at least sixty steamboats. Louden was named as one of four men the authorities were most anxious to apprehend, with Tucker, Barret, and Isaac

---

[107] Edwards, John Newman, *Shelby and His Men*, originally published 1867. McCoy is also credited with burning several steamboats, as well as going into St. Louis numerous times during the war with large quantities of Rebel mail.

Elshire.[108] Elshire was credited with the destruction of the steamer *Robert Campbell, Jr.* on September 28, 1863. In an ironic twist, one of those killed in the destruction of the *Campbell* was David Lynch, former brother-in-law of Mary Louden.

The *Sultana* arrived in Memphis near sunset on the evening of April 26. At 11 pm the boat moved across the river to the Arkansas side to take on coal. There the *Sultana* remained for two hours, leaving at 1 am to head northward up the river.

At 2 o'clock in the morning, about seven miles north of Memphis, an explosion burst through the *Sultana*. Over seventeen hundred people died; burned, scalded, and drowned. As many Union soldiers were killed that night on the river as died on the battlefield of Shiloh.[109]

A month after the destruction of the *Sultana* the Department of the Trans-Mississippi surrendered, officially ending the war in the west. Many of the Missouri Confederate leaders fled to Mexico. For those like Louden and McCoy, from Missouri, there was no general pardon. They couldn't go home. They didn't know if they could ever go home. For them, the war still did not end.

In the case of Louden, the war's official end meant nothing as regarded the hunt for him, and the death sentence awaiting him. In St. Louis, Provost Marshal James H. Baker, in one of his reports on the boatburners, added the name *Sultana* to his lists of sabotaged steamboats.

---

[108] OR, Series I—Volume XLVIII/2, pages 197. In this document "Judge Tucker" is Joseph W. Tucker, "John R. Barrett" is John Richard Barret, "Isaac Elshire" is likely Isaac Alshire, a steamboat mate, from St. Louis.

[109] Sherman, William T., *The Memoirs of General William T. Sherman by Himself*, 1875.

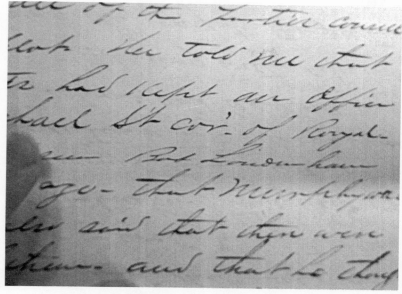

Louden in Pinkerton Report - NARA

The case of the boatburners was shifted to Washington. Allen Pinkerton was put on the case and began tracking them. One of his reports placed Louden within the area around the time in question.[110]

---

[110] NARA, RG 109, M345, roll 270, Provost Marshal's file on Joseph W. Tucker, report of Allen Pinkerton dated June 6, 1865 from New Orleans. *The report by Pinkerton from his operatives and his own investigations traces Tucker leaving Mobile, Alabama in April 1865 moving northward through Grenada, Mississippi, toward Memphis. Witnesses also placed Louden in New Orleans, and possibly Mobile, during the weeks before the report.*

Not Forgotten, Not Forgiven

The war didn't end cleanly and neatly with a single surrender as historians often would have us believe. The fighting, the anger, and the bitterness continued.

On the eve of *Sultana's* destruction, Missouri was braced for an expected invasion from Arkansas. Continued fighting was reported many places around the country.

One of the *Sultana's* survivors, Frank Kuhn of Fremont, Ohio, in an odd story told months later, said he survived the explosion uninjured. Grabbing a piece of driftwood, he eventually reached shore on the Arkansas side of the river. He awoke to find a pistol aimed at his head. Taken thirty miles away, he was turned over to a guerilla band who kept him for months. Listed among the dead, Kuhn's wife, believing she was a widow, was shocked when he arrived home.[111]

Most newspapers told far less happy stories. Few accepted or believed the idea that the *Sultana* had been destroyed by accident.

The Daily Leader, Cleveland, Ohio, on May 3, 1865 said, "The explosion of the Sultana is, to our minds, but another evidence of the malignity and barbarism of the rebellion... The frequency of accidents occurring to steamboats and railroad trains containing our soldiers, and especially Union prisoners recently released from Southern prisons, cannot have escaped public attention. Recently the burning of the General Lyon off Cape Hatteras, and the loss of over five hundred Union soldiers, horrified the nation. Here we have a new and trebly-terrible disaster, this time occurring on an inland steamer but, curiously enough, on one which, like the

---

[111] *Fremont Journal,* September 15, 1865. The story may be true. A Kuhn matches the information, and Rebel guerrillas were on the Arkansas side of the river.

Lyon, is loaded to its upmost capacity with Union soldiers. The coincidence is worth noting." The article continues, itemizing more acts of destruction, "...burning of our steamboats, and especially of those employed as transports for our Union soldiers... a part of the programme of the rebel chiefs."

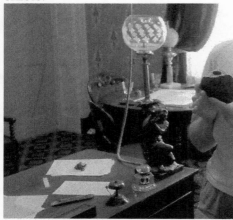

Author holding Coal Torpedo
(Thatcher replica) in J. Davis' office

That same paper, on May 25th, talked about active military campaigns in the Trans-Mississippi and attempts to bring about a surrender of the Confederate forces there, and also reports on one of the commission findings in the case of the *Sultana* disaster. The newspaper rejects the findings, as did many at the time, saying, "The report is unsatisfactory, and conveys the idea that the commission either had failed to give adequate attention to the subject, or that they were restrained by some motive from a free expression of the result of the investigation."

That commission report said the boilers and boat were in good working order, and the amount of people on the *Sultana* caused no danger to the boat, with the added note, "The evidence fully shows that the Government has transferred as many, or more, troops on boats of no greater capacity than the Sultana, frequently and with safety."[112] Insufficient water in the boilers as the cause of the explosion, was the conclusion.

---

[112] Court Martial report signed Thos. M. Brown Lieut. Col. 7th Indiana Cavalry, R. G. Rombauer, Maj. 1st Illinois Light Artillery, A. R. Eddy, Assistant Quartermaster, U.S.A. as reported in *The Highland Weekly News*, Hillsborough, Ohio, June 1, 1865

Finding unsatisfactory, answered the Ohio papers, and others around the country, "It will not satisfy the people: we hope it will not satisfy the government."

After the War

William C. Streetor returned to his career as a sign painter, and raised an ever-growing family. Absalom Grimes
resumed piloting steamboats. In 1866, Robert Louden was
dead... dead as far as St. Louis was concerned, with his wife
listed as a widow in the city directory.[113] Living nearby her,
apparently fulfilling a promise he'd made to take care of
Mary and the children when Louden's execution was expected, was younger brother Andrew Louden. "If it had
come to the worst, Mary and them would never wanted for
anything while I lived," he had said.[114]

But by the spring of 1867 Robert Louden was back, alive
and well, and in a painting business with William H. Gray.[115]
"His friends obtained a pardon for him from President
Johnson," Streetor said, "and, armed with that, he returned
to his home in St. Louis."[116]

Less than two years after the war had ended the ex-
Confederate agent and the ex-Union prison keeper were
working together in the same shop on Locust Street in St.
Louis.[117]

The war passed into history and the memory of the *Sultana* faded. The survivors remembered, though. So did
William C. Streetor.

---

[113] *1866 Edwards Annual Directory* by Edwards, Greenough & Deved.

[114] NARA, RG 109, M345, roll 170, letter from Andrew Louden to Robert
Louden, May 17, 1864.

[115] *1867 Edwards Annual Directory* by Edwards, Greenough & Deved.

[116] *St. Louis Globe-Democrat,* May 6, 1888. No pardon has yet been found
in the National Archives or any other source for Robert Louden. General
Sterling Price returned to St. Louis January 11, 1867.

[117] Ibid. / also Grimes / supported by the St. Louis business directories.

Survivors of the *Sultana* began to meet in 1885[118] and tell their stories. One year another story emerged. In 1888 a reporter of the *St. Louis Globe-Democrat,* after the publication of the statements of some survivors,[119] interviewed William C. Streetor of St. Louis. "I can give the cause of the explosion," Streetor said. "A torpedo inclosed in a lump of coal was carried aboard the steamer at Memphis and deposited in the coal pile in front of the boilers for the express purpose of causing her destruction."[120]

---

[118] Salecker.

[119] April 23, April 27, 1888, *St. Louis Globe-Democrat.*

[120] *St. Louis Globe-Democrat,* May 6, 1888.

The Coal Torpedo

The method Streetor said Louden claimed to have used was a bomb made to resemble a lump of coal. Indeed, only an hour before the explosion the *Sultana* had taken on coal. Louden had the perfect opportunity, under the cover of darkness and in the confusion of crowds of people, to place his bomb. He was experienced with such actions. "It had got to be too **** ticklish a job to set a boat afire and get away from her," Louden is quoted as saying,[121] explaining why he had used a bomb in the coal.

Thomas E. Courtenay
Richmond, 1864
The Thatcher Collection

Such a coal-shaped bomb, at that time, was known as a Courtenay Torpedo, named for its inventor, Thomas E. Courtenay. In August 1863 Courtenay, former sheriff of St. Louis county, was authorized by General Price, through Colonel Snead, to enlist a "secret-service corps, not exceeding twenty men."[122]

In March 1864, David D. Porter, Rear-Admiral Commanding Mississippi Squadron, issued General Order 184 which began, "The enemy have adopted new inventions to destroy human life and vessels in the shape of torpedoes, and an article resembling coal, which is to be

---

[121] Ibid.

[122] OR, Series I—Volume XXII/2, page 970.

placed in our coal piles for the purpose of blowing the vessels up..."[123] In addition to their shared St. Louis connections, Courtenay was involved with the same group of Confederate agents with whom Louden was associated. Both Union and Confederate records establish numerous connections. Louden would have had knowledge of, and had access to, the Courtenay Torpedo.

Coal Torpedo,
early diagram - Scharf

A Courtenay Torpedo was described by Lt. Barnes in *Submarine Warfare* as appearing to be "an innocent lump of coal, but is a block of cast-iron..."[124] The device was then covered with tar and coal powder, making it indistinguishable from the rest of the coal. J. Thomas Scharf in *History of the Confederate States Navy* says that when Courtenay Torpedoes were taken aboard Federal boats with the coal they "exploded with terrible effect on their boilers."[125]

An article datelined from New York, May 10th, 1865 reprinted in newspapers across the country, told of the discovery of a coal torpedo in the office of Jefferson Davis. "A special says the government has full details concerning Davis' bureau of torpedoes and infernal machines. Pictures of these deadly missiles were captured. Among other devices were torpedoes in the shape and appearance of lumps of steamer coal, so perfect in resemblance that they would not be readily distinguished from genuine coal. The existence of this infernal device confirms the belief that the steamer Sultana was destroyed by a torpedo in her coal."[126]

---

[123] Navy OR, Series I—Volume 26, page 184.

[124] Quoted in: Scharf, J. Thomas, *History of the Confederate States Navy*, Random House Value Publishing, Inc. reprinted 1996 from 1887 edition (hereafter "Scharf").

[125] Scharf.

[126] *Montana Post*, Virginia, Montana, May 27, 1865; *White Cloud Kansas Chief*, White Cloud, Kansas, May 25, 1865; *Daily Intelligencer*, Wheeling, Virginia, May 12, 1865; *Weekly Perrysburg Journal*, Perrysburg, Ohio,

A *New York Times* article of May 18, 1865 said, "This was the awful contrivance employed with so much success by the rebels in blowing up our transports on the Mississippi, and it is suspected that the awful disaster to the *Sultana* was accomplished by one of these diabolical things."[127]

So effective was the Courtenay Coal Torpedo at blowing up boilers, and indistinguishable from coal, that it was still in use by the OSS, the Office of Strategic Services (predecessor of the CIA) during World War II.[128]

Several witnesses in the investigations that followed the explosion also suggested the possibility of sabotage. William Rowberry—the first mate of the *Sultana*—blamed sabotage, claimed the boat was running well until the moment of the blast.[129] Captain William Postal said he had seen a fragment of what appeared to be an artillery shell among the wreckage.[130] Soon after the *Sultana* disaster the theory of a shell

---

May 24, 1865; *Cleveland Leader*, Cleveland, Ohio, May 11, 1865; numerous others.

[127] *New York Times*, May 18, 1865; *National Daily Republican*, May 19, 1865; *The Columbia Daily Phoenix*, Columbia, South Carolina, July 15, 1865. The article describes the Courtenay Torpedo found in Jefferson Davis' office after the Confederate government fled Richmond.

[128] Thatcher, Joseph M., and Thatcher, Thomas H. *Confederate Coal Torpedo: Thomas Courtenay's Infernal Sabotage Weapon*, Kenerly Press, 2011. This recently published book by two descendants of Thomas Courtenay contains a great deal of information about Courtenay and the coal torpedo, and credits the article "*Sultana*: A Case For Sabotage" as a source. In a recent conversation with Joe Thatcher, I reaffirmed, "Courtenay would not have done it," as regarded the horrific destruction of the *Sultana*, "but Robert Louden would."

[129] Potter.

[130] *Memphis Daily Bulletin*, May 2, 1865. Without reference to the *Sultana* or this comment, Grimes refers to William Postal as "our good friend." Postal was a steamboat captain, also from St. Louis, and lived there except for a few years in Memphis. One of his occupations in Memphis was coal dealer.

exploding in the furnace was "actively discussed and has many believers among experienced river men."[131]

A piece of *Sultana,* a spike in a bean field

More compelling are the descriptions of the explosion itself. A newspaper reported a witness seeing the furnace door blow open before the boilers burst.[132] Jerry O. Potter in *The Sultana Tragedy* describes the explosion "flinging live coals and splintered timber into the night sky like fireworks." Survivors mention flaming coals flying about.[133] Such descriptions suggest that the explosion may have centered in the furnace. George Byron Merrick in *Old Times on the Upper Mississippi,* in the chapter entitled "Killing Steamboats," describes how even a little explosion in the furnaces would throw "live coals over the deck."[134] Witnesses describing the 1858 destruction of the steamer *Pennsylvania,* in which four boilers exploded, make no mention of coals or burning wood from the furnace flying about, and say it took over half an hour before the boat took fire.[135]

The Courtenay coal torpedo, itself a quite small bomb, upon exploding, punctured the boiler, creating an immedi-

[131] Ibid.

[132] Ibid.

[133] Potter.

[134] Merrick, George Byron, *Old Times on the Upper Mississippi: The Recollections of a Steamboat Pilot from 1854 to 1863,* The Arthur H. Clark Company 1909.

[135] McDermott, John Francis (ed.), *Before Mark Twain: A Sampler of Old, Old Times on the Mississippi,* Southern Illinois University Press 1968. *Killed on the Pennsylvania was the brother of author Mark Twain.*

ate and much larger secondary explosion as the punctured boiler exploded from steam pressure, and often took other nearby boilers with it. Despite the frequent mentions of the *Sultana* having a boiler repaired in Vicksburg, the repaired boiler is not one that exploded.[136] Other theories, such as the boat careening, have been dismissed as unsubstantiated. Remaining accident theories, such as low water level, though they had gotten underway only hours earlier and were not running fast, rest blame on the engineers who did not survive to defend themselves and their work.

A piece of *Sultana*, a brick in a swamp. Somewhere in the swamp is the remains of one of the boilers

---

[136] Salecker. Also: civilwarstlouis.com/boatburners/salecker.htm

A Case For Sabotage

Robert Louden was certainly capable of sabotaging the *Sultana*. He had already demonstrated his willingness, and ability, to sneak aboard steamboats and destroy them, without regard to lives lost. The only factor separating the deaths on the *Sultana* from the lives he took on the *Ruth* was the sheer numbers. Louden was a calm, professional saboteur unafraid of taking risks. "He possessed bravery of a certain kind, I think, equal to that of any man who ever lived,"[137] his former jailer, Streetor, said, describing Louden.

Other boats destroyed suggest a pattern of seizing opportunity. The *Sultana* provided that opportunity coupled with a powerful personal motivation against the boat and against Mason, *Sultana's* captain. At this point in late April of 1865 no payments from Richmond could be expected yet *Sultana* was selected for destruction. On the Mississippi River the saboteurs couldn't place their torpedoes randomly as they might in some eastern areas because many of the steamer pilots and crews were sympathetic to the south and engaged in smuggling for the Confederacy throughout the war. *Sultana* was a target-of-opportunity, but it was a target.

For Louden and the other men of the Trans-Mississippi, those from Missouri in particular, the war was not over. The surrender of the Department of the Trans-Mississippi did not come until a month after the destruction of the *Sultana*. With a load of Federal soldiers on board, the steamer would have been a tempting target even without Louden's personal motivation. As for any sympathy to emaciated POWs he might have had... Louden, himself, had spent a year in a Federal prison; had a brother still a POW with whom he exchanged letters each describing how thin they had be-

---

[137] *St. Louis Globe-Democrat*, May 6, 1888.

come. His wife and father had both been Federal prisoners, persecuted and harassed. Then, too, Louden still had a death sentence hanging over him. While these Union soldiers were heading home, he had every reason to believe he would never be able to return to his home.

Would Louden have fabricated the tale he told to Streetor? It's unlikely. William C. Streetor certainly believed it. Streetor described how the confession came about:

"...at times he drank heavily, and when in his cups was disposed to talk a little too much for a man with a record like he had. It was while talking about the war, and the burning of so many boats by the Confederate agents came up in the course of the conversation. He told me that he had fired no less than half a dozen steamboats on the Mississippi. I asked him in an off-hand way what he knew about the *Sultana* explosion. Then he told me the story of the torpedo in the coal..."[138]

To tell such a tale to *Sultana* survivors was not something a man, a fellow Union veteran, like Streetor, would do had it not come from a deep belief that it was true. Streetor was a loyal Union man, a St. Louis businessman, and respected member of the Grand Army of the Republic until his death in 1920.[139]

As for Robert Louden, he had an abundance of stories about his exploits during the war sufficient to last a lifetime. He had no reason to make up others, especially a story that, even if legally pardoned for war-time actions, would most assuredly bring the personal vengeance of survivors down onto him.

There's a tone of frustration in Streetor's narrative as he talks about Louden's escaping execution in 1864, and his return to St. Louis with a pardon that would place him beyond the reach of mortal justice.

---

[138] Ibid.

[139] G. A. R. obituary of William C. Streetor, courtesy of the Missouri Historical Society.

Louden left St. Louis *very* shortly after his drunken confession to Streetor. Grudges were still being violently settled in Missouri. Louden's life in St. Louis was effectively over as soon as the story of his sabotage of the *Sultana* circulated.

Most damning of all... No one rose to Louden's defense when the story was finally published in 1888. No one who knew Louden stood up and denied the story. Absalom Grimes, Louden's wartime partner, was well-known, and had written and published numerous accounts of his own war experiences, and still lived in the area. Yet about Robert Louden and the sabotage of the *Sultana*, Grimes said not one word in Louden's defense.

Louden died of yellow fever in New Orleans in September of 1867, the same year he made his confession.[140]

There is no doubt that Streetor was talking about the same Robert Louden who was responsible for the destruction of the steamer *Ruth*; the same Robert Louden who was named as a member of the Confederate "organized boat-burners" who were responsible for the destruction of at least sixty other steamboats with numerous lives lost; the same Robert Louden who was "amusing himself" by burning government steamboats; the same Robert Louden who had joined the Liberty Fire Company under the alias Charles Deal after being released from prison as a convicted killer; the same Robert Louden who spent over a year in Gratiot Street Prison in the keeping of William C. Streetor; the same Robert Louden who later worked with Streetor; the same Robert Louden who said he would "patch his pants with the scalps of Federal soldiers"; the same Robert Louden who told Streetor he carried a torpedo aboard the *Sultana* at Memphis to destroy her.

It would take a hard, bitter, and vengeful man to do such a thing. Robert Louden was just such a man.

---

[140] *New Orleans Times Picayune*, September 22, 1867, list of yellow fever deaths between Sept. 15 and 21, 1867. "Robert Loudon, 37, Pennsylvania." *Streetor mentions his death of yellow fever in New Orleans without the date. Louden's wife remained in St. Louis until her death at age 81.*

Appendices and Documentation

St. Louis Globe-Democrat, April 23, 1888

This is the first of the three Sultana articles appearing in the St. Louis Globe-Democrat between April 23 and May 6, 1888. While it cannot be said with certainty that William C. Streetor saw this article, it certainly is likely.

Story of the Sultana

The Steamboat Explosion Which Cost
Two Thousand Lives

How a Soldiers Longing for a Drink and a
Part of Lieutenant's Epaulets Saved
The Lives of a Chicago Man
and His Companion

[From the Chicago Tribune.]

Friday next a soldierly-appearing German, aged about 45, whose features wear an expression of settled seriousness that rarely changes for an instant, will celebrate the twenty-third anniversary of the Sultana disaster. He is Edward F. Hedrick, for fifteen years a member of the Chicago police force, now proprietor of a well-ordered little saloon on the corner of Centre and Halsted streets. Besides himself there are said to be now living but five of the 2100 passengers aboard the Sultana at the time of the explosion. It will be remembered that about 400 were picked up alive, but a large proportion of that number survived their wounds and exposure only a few days, and many others swelled the roll of victims within a year or two. Mr. Hedrick served two years in the 8th New York Infantry, at the expiration of which time he enlisted at Indianapolis for three years in the 9th Indiana Cavalry. He was captured at Sliver Branch Trestle and imprisoned at Cahaba, Ala. With 2000 other Union prisoners he was exchanged and sent up the river. These passengers taken on at New Orleans, were on the boat when her boilers blew up. Mr. Hedrick recently told the story of the disaster, including the details of his own remarkable escape, for publication in the Tribune, so frankly and graphically that it is best reproduced in his own words:

"When we boarded the Sultana at Vicksburg," he began, "we were a jolly crowd. Two thousand of us had just been released from a Southern prison and we were happy. The Sultana was a regular Mississippi River packet boat of that period. A thousand passengers would have crowded her uncomfortably; with over 2000 she was like a hive of bees about to swarm.

"We steamed out of Vicksburg and moved slowly up the middle of the river. The spring floods were at their highest, the stream being in some places as much as forty miles wide. We reached Memphis at 8 o'clock in the evening. Three of my prison chums were on board—Johnny Hinckley, Montgomery Hall and John Wills—and as the Captain said he would not leave till midnight we made up our minds to land and have some fun. I'm going to tell you about this because if we hadn't gone up-town Johnny Hinckley and I would have been blown sky-high with the others. Our main object in landing was to get something to drink. But we soon discovered that the town was under martial rule and that only officers were allowed anything stronger than coffee. We were so thirsty that we went into an alleyway to reconnoiter. When we were out of sight of the street Johnny Hinckley took out of his pocket a pair of lieutenant's shoulder-straps he had picked up somewhere, put them on, and while we waited in the alley he entered the nearest saloon. He was gone quite awhile and came back a trifle unsteady, and wiping his mouth. Then I put on the shoulder straps and followed his example with equal success. By the time Hall and Wills had performed their part of the programme it was time to start back to the boat. None of us were drunk, but we were full enough to be happy and to care little whether school kept or not.

"It was just about midnight when the boat left Memphis. Everybody was in the best of spirits. There were a number of professional gamblers on board, and as we passed the cabin door I noticed that it was crowded with officers and gamblers who were playing for high stakes. We went to bunk in the middle of the middle deck, between the office and the bar room and directly over the boilers. Hall and Wills were sleepy. They rolled up in their blankets and were soon snoring. It was the last ever seen of them. I wanted to follow their example, but Johnny Hinckley wouldn't have it. He was much elated over our luck with the shoulder straps. We were both a little top-heavy, so when he insisted on going to the back end of the boat and turning into a couple of the officer's cots I readily consented. There were a great improvement over the hard floor of the deck, and we were soon sound asleep.

"The next thing I knew there was a terrible crash. The passengers were shouting and screaming and jumping into the river on all sides. I got up, and as I moved forward to see what the matter was I bumped my head against a part of the upper deck which had fallen in. Then I saw flames creeping back toward the stern and knew that the boilers had blown up. I ran back to find Hinckley, but his cot was empty. The notion of jumping into the river, as passengers were doing all around, didn't please me, so I slid down to the freight deck on one of the swinging bumpers that hung over the side. A big crowd of passengers had flocked to the stern, where a lot of mules were quartered. Many of the mules hand broken loose and were stamping up and down the deck. Several of us seized one and threw him overboard, intending to jump ourselves and let him swim us ashore. But the water was black with heads and arms of drowning passengers, and the mule sank instantly with a dozen men under and on top of him. We threw in several more, all with the same result. People were constantly jumping in and carrying others to the bottom with them. There wasn't a clear space within jumping distance in any direction. The water was rough and churned the crowd of swimmers up and down as though there were logs in a broken raft.

"All the time Capt. Mason was working bravely on the upper deck throwing planks and barrels overboard and shouting to the passengers to keep cool. Many swam ashore on what he threw into the water, but he staid aboard too long to save his own life. After awhile, when most of the passengers had thrown themselves into the river, the boat seemed to drift away from them, leaving a clear space. I had thrown several shutters over, but they had all been seized by those in the water. Finally the flames had driven the terrified mules so closely about me that I was obliged to seize a bit of plank and jump for my life. By the light of the flames I saw what I took for the shore only a few rods distant, and congratulated myself that I was getting off so easily. But it was only an island, and in spite of all I could do the current carried me past the lower end of it. There was no shore in sight. Pretty soon a half-drowned man floating by caught hold of the end of my plank. He placed his whole weight on it, and we commenced to sink together. I cursed him and said: 'Why don't you help yourself a little so we can both be saved?' But he was too exhausted. I let him have the plank, and started to swim with nothing under me. When I was nearly worn out a steamer came by picking up floating passengers so near that I thought of course she would take me on. But the wind was in the wrong direction. They couldn't hear me, and I gave myself up for lost. Just then a brandy jug floated by. I worked it under me and plucked up courage again. In this way I floated down to where the current struck the bend just above Memphis, and caught the overhanging branch of a half-submerged tree. Dozens of people had floated in just as I had, and were clinging to bushes and trees. The water was so high we couldn't touch bottom, and there was no land in sight. The blaze of the burning Sultana had been seen from Memphis, and we were presently rescued by one of the boats in search of survivors and bodies of the dead. The water was so cold that we were chilled through, but there was plenty of spirits and a blazing fire on the rescuing boat, besides piles of blankets in which we were wrapped.

"As I walked up the bank at Memphis in my blanket, almost the first person I met was Johnny Hinckley. Before jumping overboard he had secured a life preserver, and floated down to the bend without much difficultly. The people living at the principal hotel bought us new suits of clothes, and in a day or two we came North to Indianapolis. Then I lost track of Hinckley and haven't seen or heard of him since. I would like to know where he is. You see, it was nothing in the world but his shoulder-straps that saved our lives."

Story of Another Survivor

Frankfort, Ind., April 12—

James Payne, one of the few survivors of the Sultana disaster, lives in Hamilton County, this State, near Packard's Mills, and there he was found by the Tribune correspondent. Mr. Payne was a private in the 124th Indiana, which was captured by the Confederates at Spring Hill, Tenn., in 1864. He spent three months amidst the horrors of Andersonville, and was then exchanged. "Orders came to the effect that 500 men should be taken out each day to be exchanged," said Mr. Payne, "with the provision that the old men were to go first—that is, those who had been longest in the prison. But we found out that a little persuasion in the way of money had a great effect upon the officers of the prison, and as the boys of our company had succeeded in keeping a little money concealed, we bought our exchange, and consequently our company, which was now down to eleven men, got out on the first list. One of our boys went out on a dead man's name. When the dead man's name was called he answered to it. We were taken to Vicksburg, and the morning of the 1st day of May, 1865, we were marched down to the wharf to embark to be sent North and home. We lost no time in getting aboard the Sultana, as that time the largest boat on the Mississippi. She was a side-wheeler of unusual dimensions. She carried eighteen boilers. The boilers and machinery of the Sultana had been inspected at St. Louis just before her down trip, and at Vicksburg just before we started.

"We started from Vicksburg about noon. Everything went well, excepting our sickness, the result of our confinement, and the rough water, as the river was running high. We landed at Memphis at 11p.m., where we had about 400 hogsheads of sugar to unload. Here occurred my miraculous escape. A number of the boys, myself being one of them, got off here and went up into the town to see if they could get something to eat, and at least get some fresh air. A comrade, whose name I have forgotten, and myself wandered around until we heard the signal to start and then we ran for the boat, but we were too late, and the only result of our efforts was to get into the sand up to our knees. We saw that the Sultana was going to stop at some coal barges and take on some coal, and we in our desperation tried to get aboard here; but it appears that Providence was working in its own mysterious way, and we were again unsuccessful. While we were standing on the wharf, or rather in the sand, we were watching the Sultana, our hope, joy and pride, steam away, feeling our hearts sink within us.

"We watched the Sultana until she got to a point in the river where there is a small island called 'Hen and Chickens', seven miles above Memphis, where, to our horror, the boilers exploded, and then what was left of the vessel took fire, and, slowly drifting down the river, burned up. Of course a great many were killed by the explosion, but the greater part of them were either burned to death or driven by the fire into the water and drowned. Some few of the boys were able, by getting hold of some of the floating wreckage, to get ashore. One man, or boy, rather, J.W. Thompson, who was then only 18 years old, swam until he was opposite Memphis, which was seven miles, when he was picked up by a yawl. They were afraid to put out large boats until it became light, consequently no boats but skiffs and yawls were used until morning. A very dense fog also came up just immediately after the explosion. The river was very high at the time, all the bottom lands for miles on each side of the river being inundated. One soldier succeeded in getting upon a log, and also helped upon the log a lady passenger whom he found in the water, and by means of using his hands and feet as oars finally guided the log out of the channel and lodged it safely against some timber. She was, I think, a Chicago lady, and she has since handsomely rewarded him. As to the actual number saved I, of course, do not know, but I do know that it was comparatively few. John W. Thompson, whom I have named, lives now at Fisner's Switch, Ind. Lieut. Elliot is now living at Indianapolis, Ind. Matthew Wright, the man who went out on the dead man's name, is now living at Boxytown, Ind. These four men, besides myself, are all the men I think who are living, except Wesley Negley, whom I had almost forgotten."

St. Louis Globe-Democrat, April 27, 1888

This is the second of the three Sultana articles appearing in the St. Louis Globe-Democrat between April 23 and May 6, 1888. Note that it appears on the 23rd anniversary of the disaster, and talks specifically about a reunion of Sultana survivors being held in Michigan. One way or the other, this article must be the key event that lead to the publication of the revelations contained in the May 6th article.

There are two possible explanations. The first is that Streetor saw it and came forward on his own, contacting the paper to tell his story. The Sultana survivors only began meeting about 1885, during a brief time in Streetor's life when he lived outside of the St. Louis area, spending a few years in New Mexico. So it is probable this was the first notice Streetor had that such a group existed and still memorialized the event. The second possibility is that Streetor had previously shared his story with others, who when they saw the article, contacted the paper and said something like "You really ought to talk to William Streetor about this."

Sultana Survivors
Reunion at Hillsdale, Mich.
Special Dispatch to the Globe-Democrat

HILLSDALE, MICH., April 26—

Of the eighty survivors of the great Sultana disaster on April 26, 1865, Joseph Stephens, of Buffalo, N.Y., is the most interested in the re-unions of the remnant of persons now surviving that historical casualty. Stephens is one of the veterans not lost on that occasion and takes the deepest interest in the annual gatherings, at which the attendance grows appreciably less each spring. Mr. Stephens formerly lived in this place, and offered last year to pay the expenses of this year's reunion if held at his old home, which offer was accepted. The reunion is to last two days.

The programme consists of an address of welcome by the Mayor, response by the President of the society, election of officers and the spinning of yarns about the fatal day. The Grand Army veterans here and the Woman's Relief Society are taking a leading part in the entertainment of the survivors. A banquet will be given tomorrow night. Only half a dozen of the survivors have arrived up to this evening. A fair representation of the total number is looked for to arrive on the late trains tonight and early in the morning. The celebration proper takes place on the second day.

Story of a Survivor

Special Correspondence of the Globe-Democrat.

FORT WAYNE, IND., April 26.

Two veterans of the late war were distinguished yesterday above the many hundreds of their fellow solider-citizens in Fort Wayne, by receiving circular invitations to attend a meeting of the survivors of the explosion on the Mississippi River steamer Sultana, perhaps the most melancholy incident of the rebellion. The survivors have long since formed an association, and the meeting referred to is to take place at Hillsdale, Mich., on Friday, April 27, the twenty-third anniversary of the catastrophe.

The two gentlemen referred to are Louis Schirmeyer, a clothing store clerk, and Geo. H. Fredericks, a fireman on the Wabash Railway. Mr. Schirmeyer was called upon today by a Globe-Democrat representative, and related his personal experience. It was a thrilling tale, and in substance is as follows:

"I was a member of the 32d Indiana Volunteer Infantry, and had been captured at Chickamauga. I was first sent to Libby Prison, then to Pemberton Prison, next to Danville, Va., and finally to Andersonville, where I remained until the war ended. I was then taken to Vicksburg and placed on board the Sultana with 2,100 others, mostly discharged prisoners. The boat stopped at Memphis at 8 o'clock in the evening and many of us went ashore, and an opportunity for drinking was not neglected. A friend of mine had money and I filled up with beer and almost missed the boat, which resumed its course at midnight. In fact, I was the last to cross the gang plank, which was at once drawn in after me. In the vast crowd it was difficult to find a place to lie down, but I found one on the top-most deck, just in front of the pilot house. Here I fell into a deep sleep. I was awakened by the noise of a terrific explosion of the boilers, and found myself being hurled upward through the air. I must have gone up 20 or 25 feet. In falling I struck the shattered pilot house. My face was cut and bleeding, and my hair was half singed off by a flame that burst over me. It was a rude awakening. I swung myself down a rope that hung over the boat's side, and from a perch on the lower deck peered out into the river. The night was moonless, but the flames spread a bright gleam over the swollen stream. Never can I forget that scene. The heads of the people in the water were so numerous that it seemed as if an apple thrown in any direction must have surely hit one of them. Some cursed, some prayed, all cried out for help. Every few minutes a hand would be uplifted helplessly, and the next moment its owner would be swept out of my sight. The flames grew hotter, and approached more nearly. My place of observation could be held but a little longer. To remain would be to burn to death. To jump would be to drown, for I was an indifferent swimmer. The increasing heat decided me. I sprang into the water. A mattress, which had been thrown from the cabin deck, floated by me. Two Irishmen seized it. I cautioned them not to bear their entire weight upon it, but they gave no heed and were soon sprawled on its top. The mattress became water-soaked and sunk. The two Irishmen sunk with it. Scenes like this were constantly occurring. I paddled on as best I could. At last, when my strength was almost exhausted, I was struck from behind, and turning about, grasped a floating piece of timber that had probably been a deck support. I threw my arms over it, and in an hour had floated into the branches of a tree that overhung the swollen river. I clambered to a place of safety. Four others found places in the tree. Here we remained until daylight, when one of the many boats that had been sent up from Memphis for the relief of the survivors approached near enough to hear our cries. We were lifted on board. I fainted at once. In three days I was able to pursue my journey by another steamer to Cairo, and at Indianapolis I received an ovation and was mustered out."

St. Louis Globe-Democrat, May 6, 1888

This is the last of the three Globe-Democrat Sultana articles appearing between April 23 and May 6, 1888. It is truly amazing this article seems to have been completely lost to history until rediscovered as part of our investigation.

Unfortunately, this article was practically the last thing we found instead of the first. Almost all of the revelations found in this article had been discovered by us from other sources before we ever saw it. We had talked for months about our case being built around the fact of the centrality of St. Louis—as opposed to Vicksburg or Memphis—to the "sabotage theory." More and more we convinced ourselves that if the Memphis papers had published Streetor's story, then there had to be some significant mention of it in the St. Louis papers. These two men were just too well known there for the St. Louis papers to have taken no notice whatever of Streetor's accusation against Louden.

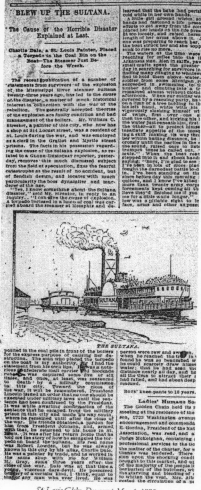

St. Louis Globe-Democrat, May 6, 1888

BLEW UP THE SULTANA

The Cause of the Horrible Disaster
Explained at Last.

Charlie Dale, a St. Louis Painter, Placed
a Torpedo in the Coal Bin on the
Boat—The Steamer Just Be-
fore the Wreck.

The recent publication of a number of statements from survivors of the explosion of the Mississippi River steamer Sultana twenty-three years ago, has led to the cause of the disaster, a matter of much historical interest in connection with the war of the rebellion. The generally accepted theories of the explosion are faulty condition and bad management of the boilers. Mr. William C. Streetor, a painter of this city, who now has a shop at 314 Locust street, was a resident of St. Louis during the war, and was employed as a clerk in the Gratiot and Myrtle street prisons. The facts in his possession regarding the cause of the Sultana explosion, as related to a GLOBE-DEMOCRAT reporter, yesterday, removes this much discussed subject from the field of speculation, fixes the fearful catastrophe as the result of no accident, but of fiendish design, and locates with much particularity the boss dynamiter and murderer of the age.

"Yes, I know something about the Sultana disaster," said Mr. Streeter, in reply to an inquiry. "I can give the cause of explosion. A torpedo in a lump of coal was carried aboard the steamer at Memphis and deposited in the coal pile in front of the boilers for the express purpose of causing her destruction. The man who placed the torpedo on the boat is my authority, for I had the statement from his own lips. He was a notorious Confederate mail carrier and blockade runner, was captured some five or six times, and once, at least, was sentenced to death by a military commission in this city. Toward the close of the war, it will be remembered, President Lincoln issued an order that no one should be executed under military laws until the sentence had been confirmed by the President. It was while awaiting confirmation of the sentence that he escaped from the military prison in this city and made his way South, where he remained until after the close of the war. His friends obtained a pardon for him from President Johnson, and, armed with that, he returned to his home in St. Louis. It was after his return home that he told me the story of how he smuggled the torpedo on board the Sultana. His real name was Robert Lowden, but he was always known in this city by his alias, Charlie Dale.

He was a painter by trade, and he worked in the same shop with me for William H. Gray, some three years after the close of the war. Dale was at that time a young, vigorous dare-devil. He possessed bravery of a certain kind, I think, equal to that of any man who ever lived. He was cool and calculating in his disposition, but at times he drank heavily, and when in his cups was disposed to talk a little too much for a man with a record like he had. It was while he was drinking one day that he and I got to talking about the war, and the burning of so many boats by the Confederate agents came up in the course of the conversation. He told me that he had fired no less than half a dozen steamboats on the Mississippi. I asked him in an off-hand way what he knew about the Sultana explosion. Then he told me the story of the torpedo in the coal, and, using his own expression, "It had got to be too—ticklish a job to set the boat afire and get away from her."

Out of a hundred other of Dale's daring exploits during the war one in particular impressed me forcibly as showing the character of this remarkable man. It was accomplished while the federal fleet was lying between Memphis and Vicksburg. Dale had escaped from prison in this city, and was on his way South. He was in a quandary for several days as to how he was going to get through the Federal lines. Finally he hit upon a plan and it was successful. He got a coffin at Memphis, calked it up with white lead, and launched it on the Mississippi. Then he laid himself out in the ghastly looking boat and floated down the stream. He passed the Government gunboats at night, and two or three times when the current of the stream drifted the coffin up against the hulls of the boats he reached out with his hands, pushed his craft clear and landed in the morning safe within the Confederate lines.

"Before the war Dale was a member of the old Liberty volunteer fire company in this city and was well known to a great many people living here now. He died in New Orleans during the yellow fever epidemic along in the latter part of the '60s. But to return to the Sultana explosion. I have read carefully all the information I could find about it, and from the character of the explosion I have been led to believe that Charley Dale's story of the torpedo is true."

[Article continues with scenes from rescue of survivors. . .]

Memphis Daily Appeal, May 8, 1888

This is the Memphis article most commonly cited in previous books and articles when mentioning the possible sabotage of the Sultana.

EXPLOSION OF THE SULTANA

Another Theory of the Cause Advanced by a St. Louis Man

St. Louis, Mo, May 7 -- The awful explosion on the steamer Sultana near Memphis twenty-three years ago, in which nearly 2,000 Union soldiers lost their lives, has always been a mystery. The survivors at their reunion have recently made a number of statements regarding the affair, but the most sensational story has been told by a resident of this city, William C. Streeter. His statement fixes the explosion as the result of design. He claims that a noted Confederate blockade runner and mail carrier named Robert Lowden, better known during the war as Charles Dale, was the author of the terrible disaster. Streeter claims that Lowden told him, after the close of the war, that while the Sultana lay at the Memphis wharf, he smuggled aboard a large lump of coal in which was concealed a torpedo. This he deposited on the fuel pile in front of the boilers for the express purpose of causing the destruction of the boat.

Whether the responsibility for the awful crime rests solely with Lowden, or whether he was acting under the direction of others, Streeter is unable to say. Lowden had an adventurous career, being captured several times while running blockades, and once narrowly escaped execution. What has become of him is not known.

The Boatburners in the Official Records

*(occasional emphasis added in **bold** by the author)*

Official Records «13 R R--VOL XLVIII, PT II»
HEADQUARTERS DEPARTMENT OF THE MISSOURI,
OFFICE OF PROVOST-MARSHAL-GENERAL,
Saint Louis, Mo., April 25, 1865.
 Hon. C. A. DANA,
  Assistant Secretary of War, Washington, D.C.:
SIR: I have the honor to state that in the month of January last I
obtained information from various sources of the presence, in
Saint Louis and other river cities, of a number of men employed
by the rebel authorities to destroy Government property and
steam-boats. I gave immediate attention to the matter, using all
the means at my command to find and secure the parties, with so
much success that early in February 1 was enabled to make the
arrest of ten of them, among whom was one Edward Frazor, the
leader. One of the parties implicated at once made a full confession, upon the understanding that he should not be prosecuted. I
then preferred charges against Frazor, intending to make his the
test case, and turned him over with the evidence to a military
commission. Circumstances over which I had no control have
delayed the trial, and Frazor, probably becoming weary of his
imprisonment, and hoping that he might be reprieved by giving
evidence against his accomplices, a few days since made a confession of his connection with the boat burners, which not only
corroborates the information I had already procured, but throws
additional light on the matter.
From this statement it appears that Frazor went, in company with
others, to Richmond in the summer of 1864, and was introduced
to Mr. Seddon, the Secretary of War. His account of what occurred at that interview is as follows:

 At Richmond, Clark introduced me to the Secretary of
 War, Secretary Seddon. Clark told his business, when he
 sent us to the Secretary of State, J.P. Benjamin. I believe
 he looked our statement over and took time to consider.
 * * * The next day I went there, and Mr. Benjamin asked
 me if I knew all these claims for destroying U. S. property
 were right and correct. I told him they were, as far as I
 knew. He then offered $30,000 in greenbacks to settle. I

told him I could not take that. Then he said he would take
time to study again.

*   *   *   *

Benjamin next offered $35,000 in gold. Then Clark went
to see him, and before he went I told him to get all he
could, but not take less than the $35,000 down and get all
the more he could. When he came back he said he had
taken the $35,000 down and $15,000 on deposit, payable
in four months from date, provided those claims of the
Louisville matter (burning of Government medical stores
last year) were all right. I think that is the way the receipt
read. I went over to Benjamin's to sign the receipt, and
while I was there the President, Jefferson Davis, sent for
me. I went in to see him with Mr. Benjamin. Mr. Davis
was talking about sending men up here to destroy the long
bridge, near Nashville. He asked me if I knew anything
about it--knew where it was. I told him I did. He asked
me which would be the best route to send men up here to
do it. I told him I thought it was rather dangerous to send
men up here who had never been here. He wanted to
know if I would not take charge of it. I told [him] yes,
provided he would stop all men from coming up here, as
they would only hinder the work. He said he would do it,
and wanted to know if I wanted any men from there to
help me. I said I didn't. Benjamin said the pay would be
$400,000 for burning the bridge. After we got all ready to
leave Mr. Benjamin gave us a draft for $34,800 in gold on
Columbia, S.C.

* * * Clark got passes from the Secretary of War, twelve
or thirteen in all.

The party, some six in all, left Richmond, drew the money, and
started for Memphis. At Mobile they were arrested, but upon tel-
egraphing the fact to Jeff. Davis, he ordered General Taylor,
commanding the department, to release them, which was done,
and they proceeded on their way, entering our lines near Memphis. At this place they separated, going in various directions.
The names and residences of the principal men engaged in this
infamous pursuit, which has resulted in the destruction of so
much valuable property and life, are as follows:

No. Name. Residence.
Remarks.

1 Tucker, Judge(a) Mobile, Ala
Chief of this service under the Secretary of War.

2 Majors, Minor
Next in rank to Tucker, and chief of this service in our lines.....

3 Barrett, Hon. John R(b) Saint *Louis,* Mo
In charge of "land operations;" can get him any time.

4 Harwood, S. B do
Can arrest him any time.

5 Frazor, Edward do
In Gratiot Prison..

6 Clark, Thomas L Grenada, Miss
Supposed to be in rebel lines.

7 Irwin,William Louisville, Ky.....

8 Dillingham, Henry
....Inside our lines.

9 Fox, Harrison Saint Louis, Mo ....

10 Stinson, --Mobile, Ala ....

11 Roberts, Kirk do ....

12 **Louden, Robert Saint Louis, Mo**
Under sentence of death. Escaped from Lieutenant Post
while being transferred from Gratiot to Alton Military Prison.
Last heard from in New Orleans; supposed to be in rebel lines
east of Mississippi.

13 Elshire, Isaac (c)....
In Gratiot Prison last year, but released for want of evidence;
supposed to be inside rebel lines east of Mississippi River.

14 Raison, John........

15 Mitchell, Peter Saint Louis, Mo.
Inside our lines.

16 Murphy, William New Orleans, La
Came voluntarily and exposed the others; afterward left suddenly;
am looking for him.

17 O'Keife,--Natchez, Miss ....

18 Triplett, -- ....

19 Parks, John G Near Memphis,Tenn.
In Gratiot Prison.

The foregoing list contains the names of the principal men only, as far as I have been able to ascertain them, and does not embrace any merely supposititious cases. A number of those most needed, it will be observed, are in territory which until recently has been occupied by the rebel army, where it will require your authority to operate. I therefore respectfully suggest that you order the commanding generals of the several departments to ascertain whether any of the parties above named are within the limits of their jurisdiction; and if so, to arrest and forward them to Saint Louis without delay.

It would be impossible to obtain a correct account of the property destroyed by these parties during the war, but the following list has been traced to one or the other of the men whose names are given above:

Name.	Where burned.	Date.
City of Madison	Vicksburg, Miss	August, 1863.
Champion	Memphis, Tenn	Do.
Robert Campbell, Jr	Milliken's Bend	September 28, 1863
Imperial	Saint Louis, Mo	Do.
Hiawatha	do	Do.
Post Boy	do	Do.
Jesse K. Bell	do	Do.
Chancellor		
Forest Queen		
Catahoula	Saint Louis, Mo	September, 1863.
Wharf-boats	Mound City, Ill	Do.
Do	Cairo, Ill	Do.
Small tow-boat	Memphis,Tenn	Do.

Since the outbreak of the rebellion to the present time over seventy steam-boats owned in Saint Louis have been destroyed by fire alone. Of this number only nine have been fired by rebels in arms, and there can be little doubt but the greater portion of the balance were fired by the above or similar emissaries of the rebel government.

By direction of Major-General Dodge:

I am, sir, very respectfully, your obedient servant,

**J. H.
BAKER,**

Colonel and Provost-Marshal-General, Dept. of the Missouri.

[First indorsement.]

HEADQUARTERS DEPARTMENT OF THE MISSOURI,
Saint Louis, April 26, 1865.

Respectfully forwarded to the Assistant Secretary of War, Washington, D.C.

I consider it important that these parties be brought to justice, and would suggest that good detectives be sent to Richmond and Mobile to arrest the parties named as in the rebel service and obtain further evidence. There is no doubt of the guilt of the parties. They were in the habit of burning boats, store-houses, &c., taking to Richmond papers with full account of burning, there filing affidavits, and on that receiving their pay. They then came into our lines and squandered the money, which brought them to our notice, and on making arrests the entire *modus operandi* was divulged. We have a large amount of testimony in the case, but desire to obtain more proof before we go to trial, and, if possible, get all the parties.

**G. M.
DODGE,**

Major-General.

[Second indorsement.]
WAR DEPARTMENT,
BUREAU OF MILITARY JUSTICE,
May 16, 1865.

Respectfully returned to the Secretary of War.

It appears from the within report of Col. J. H. Baker, provost-marshal-general, Department of the Missouri, that two members of the conspiracy engaged in destroying Government boats and property on the Mississippi River, principally in 1863, have confessed that they were employed by the rebel authorities and that they were paid at Richmond by the rebel Secretary of State, and that in one instance one of them was personally engaged and contracted with by Davis himself to destroy valuable property in the use of our Government. The confession of Frazor to this effect is fully detailed by Colonel Baker, and would appear to be most conclusive.

Colonel Baker presents a list of names of the parties connected with this conspiracy (by which, as he estimates, some sixty boats were consumed and in some cases lives of soldiers, &c., were destroyed), and urges that the commanding officers of the various departments be ordered to ascertain which, if any, of the individuals named are within their jurisdiction and to arrest such as are found and send them to Saint Louis for trial. Major-General Dodge further advises, in his indorsement, that detectives be sent to Richmond and Mobile to arrest parties supposed to be commorant there, and to obtain further evidence. These recommendations are concurred in.

The subject is regarded as one of great importance, especially as illustrating the fact that Davis and other leaders of the rebellion have been the principals in this and other similar detestable and treasonable enterprises executed by men who were merely their hirelings. It is esteemed to be **of the greatest consequence that such men, especially as Judge Tucker, John R. Barrett, Isaac Elshire, Louden, and other conspicuous members of the conspiracy, should be apprehended** as promptly as possible, and that all of the gang who can be found should be tried together by

military commission for a treasonable conspiracy in the interest
of the rebellion. It is further recommended that certified copies
of all the affidavits and other written evidence in the case be required to be forwarded to the War Department for the use or
reference of the executive officers of the Government.

**A. A.
HOSMER,**

Major and Judge-Advocate. *(In the absence of the Judge-
Advocate. General.)*

[Third indorsement.]

WAR DEPARTMENT,
May 26, 1865.

Respectfully referred to the Adjutant-General. The recommendations of the Judge-Advocate-General, Colonel Baker, and
General Dodge are approved, and will be carried into effect
without delay. By order:

**JAS. A.
HARDIE,**

Inspector-General U.S. Army.

SERIES II--VOLUME VIII [S# 121]
HEADQUARTERS DEPARTMENT OF THE MISSOURI,
April 26, 1865.

Maj. Gen. E. R. S. CANBY,

Comdg. Military Division of West Mississippi, New Orleans, La.:
GENERAL: I have the honor to request that you will cause the
arrest of the following parties who are believed to be within the
limits of your division and send them to this city: Judge Tucker,
Mobile, formerly an editor and politician in Missouri; Minor
Majors, whereabouts unknown; Thomas L. Clark, Grenada,
Miss; Isaac Elshier, New Orleans; John Raison, whereabouts
unknown; **Bob Louden, New Orleans, formerly of Saint Louis**; ------ O'Keif, Natchez, Miss.; ------ Stinson and Kirk Roberts,
Mobile, Ala. **These parties have all been employed in the rebel secret service to burn steam-boats and Government
property**. I have some of their accomplices in prison here, some
of whom have given detailed statements of their connection with
the gang. From these confessions it appears that the boat and
bridge-burning operations were conducted under the immediate
supervision of Jeff Davis, Judah P. Benjamin., and Mr. Seddon.
The names above given are those of some of the principals
against whom I have the most ample evidence of guilt.
By direction of Major-General Dodge:

**J. H.
BAKER,**

Colonel and Provost-Marshal General.

O.R.--SERIES I--VOLUME XLIII/1 [S# 91]
CONFEDERATE CORRESPONDENCE, ORDERS, AND RETURNS RELATING SPECIALLY TO OPERATIONS IN NORTHERN VIRGINIA, WEST VIRGINIA, MARYLAND, AND PENNSYLVANIA, SEPTEMBER 1, 1864, TO DECEMBER 31, 1864.--#4

TORONTO, *C. W., December* 3, 1864.
(Received February 13, 1865.--*J. P. B.)*
     Hon. J.P. BENJAMIN,
        Secretary of State:
SIR: Several times have I attempted to send you communications, but I have no assurance that any one of them has been received. I have relaxed no effort to carry out the objects the Government had in view in sending me here. I had hoped at different times to have accomplished more, but still I do not think my mission has been altogether fruitless. At all events we have afforded the Northwestern States the amplest opportunity to throw off the galling dynasty at Washington and openly to take ground in favor of States' rights and civil liberty.

[portion deleted]

     Soon after I reached Canada a Mr. Minor Major visited me and represented himself as an accredited agent from the Confederate States to destroy steam-boats on the Mississippi River, and that his operations were suspended for want of means. I advanced to him $2,000 in Federal currency, and soon afterward several boats were burned at Saint Louis, involving an immense loss of property to the enemy. He became suspected, as he represented to me, of being the author of this burning, and from that time both he and his men have been hiding and consequently have done nothing.

[portion deleted]

     Very respectfully, your obedient servant,

                                                 J. THOMPSON.

O.R.--SERIES IV--VOLUME III [S# 129]
**CORRESPONDENCE, ORDERS, REPORTS, AND
RETURNS OF THE CONFEDERATE AUTHORITIES
FROM JANUARY 1, 1864, TO THE END.--#7**

DEMOPOLIS, *February* 27, 1864.
   His Excellency President DAVIS,
   Richmond:
This will be handed you by Mr. Minor Major, a citizen of Missouri, who comes to me properly authenticated. He has been
employed in the work of destroying the property of the enemy
on the rivers, and is a member of an organization of a formidable
character extending through the North, of which I have known
for some time past and of which you have heard. He goes to
Richmond on matters connected with his work, and I think you
will be interested in hearing from him of the associations with
which he is connected. Properly used, these associations could
be of great value to our cause.
Respectfully, your obedient servant,
                                                    L. POLK,
       Lieutenant-General.
[Indorsement.]
Respectfully referred to the Honorable Secretary of War.
                                                    **S. R.
                                                    M[ALLORY],**
       Secretary.

O.R.-- SERIES I--VOLUME XXIV/3 [S# 38]
**Correspondence, Orders, And Returns Relating To Opera-
tions In Mississippi And West Tennessee (And Those In
Arkansas And Louisiana Connected With The Siege Of
Vicksburg) From January 20 To August 10, 1863.
CONFEDERATE CORRESPONDENCE, ETC.--#19**

DALTON, *January* 31, 1864.
       Hon. JAMES A. SEDDON, *Secretary of War:*
SIR: I have had the honor to receive the letter of the Secretary of
the Treasury to the President, dated January 9, with your indorsement, dated 11th.
During the siege of Vicksburg, Governor Pettus proposed to me
the adoption of a plan suggested by Judge Tucker, to be executed under that gentleman's direction, to cut off supplies from the
besieging army. He required $20,000 to inaugurate it. I drew a
check for that sum on The assistant treasurer in Mobile, in favor
of Governor Pettus, who indorsed it to Judge Tucker. After con-
siderable delay, caused by reference of the matter to the

Treasury Department, the money was paid. While I remained in Mississippi, Judge Tucker was, I believe, using this money against the enemy's navigation of the river. About the end of October, I wrote an explanation of the case to the Secretary of the Navy, to be delivered by Judge Tucker, who had large claims against that Department for enemy's property destroyed on the water.

This sum was not a part of that transferred to me by Commander [Samuel] Barron, all of which was returned by me to the Navy Department.

Most respectfully, your obedient servant,

> J. E.
> **JOHNSTON.**

O.R.-- SERIES I--VOLUME XXIV/3 [S# 38]
Correspondence, Orders, And Returns Relating To Operations In Mississippi And West Tennessee (And Those In Arkansas And Louisiana Connected With The Siege Of Vicksburg) From January 20 To August 10, 1863.
UNION CORRESPONDENCE, ETC.--#24

CAIRO, *ILL., August* 6, 1863.

Maj. Gen. H. W. HALLECK, *General-in- Chief:*
The steamer Ruth, on her trip down the river with cargo of stores, and between two and three millions of money, in charge of eight paymasters, for Vicksburg, burned last night between Cairo and Columbus. I have sent the steamer Crawford to render all assistance possible, and requested Fleet Captain Pennock, commanding navy station at Cairo, to make all efforts for the recovery of the money boxes. The wreck is in Lucas Bend, 4 miles below Norfolk. Between 20 and 30 lives are supposed to be lost.

> **ASBOTH.**

O.R.--SERIES III--VOLUME III [S# 124]
CORRESPONDENCE, ORDERS, REPORTS, AND RETURNS OF THE UNION AUTHORITIES FROM JANUARY 1 TO DECEMBER 31, 1863.(*)--# 39

PAYMASTER-GENERAL'S OFFICE,
Washington, November 3, 1863.

Hon. E. M. STANTON,
Secretary of War:
SIR: I have the honor to submit herewith a report of the transactions of the Pay Department of the Army for the fiscal year ending June 30, 1863, and of its present condition:

[portion deleted]

On the 4th of August last the steamer Ruth, having on board a party of paymasters and the sum of about $2,600,000 in U.S. notes for the payment of the army of General Grant, was destroyed by fire on the Mississippi River below Cairo, and all the money on board consumed. The strictest investigations and the inquiry of a board of officers, appointed by yourself, leave no doubt that these funds were entirely destroyed. Being in U.S. notes, there is no actual loss to the Government, as they can be replaced by issuing new notes.

I would respectfully urge that Congress be requested to pass an act for the relief of the paymasters who are now charged on the books of the accounting officers of the Treasury with the funds thus destroyed.

[portion deleted]

I have the honor to be, sir, very respectfully, your obedient servant,

**T. P.
ANDREWS,**

Paymaster- General.

O.R.-- SERIES I--VOLUME XXII/2 [S# 33]
Correspondence, Orders, And Returns Relating To Operations In Missouri, Arkansas, Kansas, The Indian Territory, And Department Of The Northwest, From January 1 To December 31, 1863.
CONFEDERATE CORRESPONDENCE, ETC.--#8

SPECIAL ORDERS, No. 135.
HEADQUARTERS DISTRICT OF ARKANSAS
Little Rock, *August* 18, 1863.
* * * * * * * * *
*

VI. **Thomas E. Courtenay, esq., is, by direction of the lieutenant-general commanding the Trans. Mississippi Department, authorized to enlist a secret-service corps,** not exceeding 20 men, to be employed by him, subject to the orders of the district commander.
* * * * *

By command of Major-General Price:

**THOS. L.
SNEAD,**

Assistant Adjutant-General.

O.R.-- SERIES I--VOLUME XXII/2 [S# 33]

Correspondence, Orders, And Returns Relating To Operations In Missouri, Arkansas, Kansas, The Indian Territory, And Department Of The Northwest, From January 1 To December 31, 1863.
UNION CORRESPONDENCE, ETC.--#25

OFFICE OF CHIEF QUARTERMASTER,
Saint Louis, October 5, 1863.
      Maj. Gen. H. W. HALLECK,
        General-in-Chief, Washington, D.C.:
GENERAL: The continued destruction of steamboats, by fire, on these waters is assuming a very alarming feature. Unquestionably there is an organized band of incendiaries, members of which are stationed at every landing. It is a current report here that the Confederate Government has secretly offered a large reward for the destruction of our steamers. Already some fourteen first-class boats have been burned, and this is equivalent to 10 per cent. of the whole river transportation. Increase of watchmen and extra vigilance do not seem to arrest this insidious enemy. The incendiary, when it serves his purpose, becomes one of the crew, and thus secures himself from detection. I apprehend that there are disloyal men in disguise in the employ of every steamer, and it will be difficult to eliminate them. General Schofield is alive to the importance of some extra official action. What would you advise?
Very respectfully, your obedient servant,

                                   ROBT.
                                 ALLEN,
      Chief Quartermaster

(*excerpts from a Federal summary of the Order of American Knights investigation*)

O.R.--SERIES II--VOLUME VII [S# 120]
    UNION & CONFED. CORRESPONDENCE, ORDERS, ETC., RELATING TO PRISONERS OF WAR AND STATE FROM APRIL 1, 1864, TO DECEMBER 31, 1864.-- #38

In Missouri regular mail communication was for a long period maintained through the agency of the order from Saint Louis to Price's army, by means of which private letters as well as official dispatches between him and the grand commander of Missouri were regularly transmitted.

Eighth. Destruction of Government property. There is no doubt that large quantities of Government property have been burned or otherwise destroyed by the agency of the order in different localities. At Louisville, in the case of the steamer Taylor, and on the Mississippi River steamers belonging to the United States have been burned at the wharves, and generally when loaded with Government stores. Shortly before the arrest of Bowles, the senior of the major-generals of the order in Indiana,' he had been engaged in the preparation of "Greek fire," which it was supposed would be found serviceable in the destruction of public property. It was generally understood in the councils of the order in the State of Kentucky that they were to be compensated for such destruction by the rebel Government, by receiving a commission of 10 per cent. of the value of the property so destroyed, and that this value was to be derived from the estimate of the loss made in each case by Northern newspapers.

O.R.--SERIES I--VOLUME XLVIII/1 [S# 101]
UNION CORRESPONDENCE, ORDERS, AND RETURNS RELATING TO OPERATIONS IN LOUISIANA AND THE TRANS-MISSISSIPPI STATES AND TERRITORIES, FROM JANUARY 1, 1865, TO MARCH 31, 1865.(*)--#37

HEADQUARTERS DEPARTMENT OF THE MISSOURI,
OFFICE OF PROVOST-MARSHAL-GENERAL,
Saint Louis, March 29, 1865.
 Brig. Gen. LEWIS B. PARSONS,
  Assistant Quartermaster-General, Washington, D.C.:
GENERAL: Immediately upon entering on my duties here as provost-marshal-general my attention was drawn to the numerous cases of steam-boat burning by rebel emissaries on the Mississippi River and its tributaries. I received direct information from several quarters of the existence of organized bands sent here by the chiefs of the so-called Confederate Government to carry out their designs on our western transportation. The records of this office also furnished evidence, collected by my predecessors, to the same effect. Believing that an energetic effort on my part would result in exposing and securing some of the parties engaged in this infamous and murderous business, and perhaps of breaking it up altogether, I began a secret and thorough investigation of the matter here in this city, gradually enlarging the field of my operations until I had detectives in several of the principal river cities in other departments, and on one

occasion I sent my agents beyond the lines. My most sanguine expectations were more than realized. I procured not only evidence of the existence of these organized bands, but also the names of the leaders of some of them, and the *modus operandi* of carrying on their work, together with the names and location of men inside the rebel lines who have the immediate charge of it, under the Secretary of War. Some of the parties have been arrested and are now in Gratiot Street prison awaiting trial, among whom is the leader of a gang operating in Louisville, Cairo, Memphis, and **Saint Louis, with headquarters here**. The evidence shows that these men were at Richmond and Mobile last summer; that they had passes signed by James A. Seddon, Secretary of War, to enable them to move through rebel territory; that they crossed the lines in Mississippi within twenty-five miles of Memphis and subsequently scattered in various directions; that they brought a large amount of gold from Richmond, which it was understood among themselves was to pay for the burning of certain Government property at Louisville and Cairo last summer, &c. Charges have been drawn up against some of them, and their cases will be brought before a military commission at an early day. I am now on the track of other parties in New Orleans, Saint Louis, Mississippi, and Ohio, but at this juncture, just as I have got the matter fairly in hand, and have become acquainted with the names of parties, their haunts, and operations, the money at my command has given out and I am powerless to pursue the investigation further without means are furnished me for that purpose. From the knowledge I have acquired of boat burners and their operations, from New Orleans to Saint Paul, and from beyond the Mississippi to New York and the Atlantic coast, from the favorable location in which I am now placed to gain information of this character, and from having agents already trained to the service at my command, I am satisfied that I could, if the only draw back, the lack of money, was removed, not only effectually break up boat burning in the West, but also bring many of the boat burners and their abettors to punishment.

I have the honor to be, general, very respectfully, your obedient servant,

J. H.
BAKER,
Colonel and Provost-Marshal-General, Department of the Missouri.

[First indorsement.i
HEADQUARTERS DEPARTMENT OF THE MISSOURI,
Saint Louis, March 31, 1865.
Respectfully forwarded to Brig. Gen. L. B. Parsons, assistant quartermaster-general, Washington, D. C.

I have made requisition on the Secretary of War for $10,000, as secret-service fund to be used in this and other cases. We stand in great need of the money, and have no means of obtaining it in this department.

G. M.
DODGE,
Major-General, Commanding

[Second indorsement.]
QUARTERMASTER-GENERAL'S OFFICE,
Washington, D.C., April 18, 1865.
Respectfully referred to Hon. C. A. Dana, Assistant Secretary of War.
By order of the Quartermaster-General:

LEWIS B.
PARSONS,
Colonel and Chief of Rail and River Transportation.

O.R.-- SERIES I--VOLUME XXXII/2 [S# 58]
UNION CORRESPONDENCE, ORDERS, AND RETURNS RELATING TO OPERATIONS IN KENTUCKY, SOUTHWEST VIRGINIA, TENNESSEE, MISSISSIPPI, ALABAMA, AND NORTH GEORGIA, FROM JANUARY 1, 1864, TO FEBRUARY 29, 1864.--#1

HEADQUARTERS SIXTEENTH ARMY CORPS,
Memphis, Tenn., January 2, 1864.
    Col. J. C. KELTON,
    Asst. Adjt. Gen., Hdqrs. of the Army, Washington, D.C.:
SIR: I have the honor of forwarding to the General-in-Chief statements of one of my agents just from Mobile. I think them accurate, and so submit them.
Your obedient servant,

S. A.
HURLBUT,
Major-general.

[Inclosure.]
DECEMBER 31, 1863.
    Force at Mobile, two regiments home-guard exempts, Cantey's brigade cavalry, one battalion light artillery, heavy artillerists to man the batteries, two battalions marines, wooden steam-vessels of war Gaines and Morgan (twelve guns each, 30-pounder smooth-bores); ram Baltic (unwieldy, one Blakely, two light columbiads, two brass pivot Parrotts); Huntsville and Tuscaloosa (four 30-pounders each on both sides, 11-inch Brooke on pivot

in bow, and 11-inch Blakely on pivot astern, plated 4-inch slab-iron); two floating batteries (four square sides, plated railroad iron, armed like last two named vessels, but armament not all in): ram Tennessee (screw propeller, 11 knots, three thicknesses slab-iron, 9-inch oak, 14 of pine, armament to be two 10-inch columbiads on larboard and starboard; one large Brooke gun in bow on pivot, three ports and one in stern; very formidable craft afloat, and to take in armament outside the bar). No heavy guns mounted on north and few on west side of the city in the fortifications; eight batteries heavy artillery line the harbor entrance; a new fort being erected at Grant's Pass, under cover of gun-boats; shells of the fleet pass over Fort Morgan. Steam tug Boston to go on piratical cruise (one 3-inch Parrott and one 12-pounder howitzer). In case of attack re-enforcements to come down Mobile and Ohio Railroad from Enterprise and Meridian; at former place 3,000 paroled prisoners. French's division having gone to Georgia four weeks ago; at latter point decimated Missouri brigade, captured [at] Vicksburg. Polk's command consists of Loring's corps, in winter quarters at Canton, and Jackson's division of cavalry, out toward Big Black.

On 24th one brigade of cavalry started to march toward Grenada. Same day cavalry at Panola marched northward. Railroad bridge over Pearl River being reconstructed; trains on Meridian road run to Brandon and the river; on Mississippi Central, Grenada to 12 miles of Jackson. Bridge over Yallabusha not being rebuilt, and one locomotive north running between Panola and Grenada. Force under Polk probably be sent to Georgia; infantry, estimated, 5,000; Hardee's effective, 32,000; Johnston to assume command. Three or four light batteries, breech-loading 3-pounders, to fire incendiary shell, to operate along river about Austin. **Steam-boat burners under J. W. Tucker, Mobile; agents all over the river; principal disbursing agent, Major Pleasants, at Senatobia. Drafts and checks to pay-agents paid in Memphis and Saint Louis.** At latter point man named Hedenberg, in Homeyer's commission house, concerned somehow. Informer, an old dealer named Prescott, went out Christmas week to Elam's, 12 miles on Holly Ford road, probably on this business. **Parties concerned frequently come near the lines of Memphis and return south.** Cotton brought into Memphis to raise funds for secret agents. **Gaines one of the burners, and probably Loudon.** Forrest to be maintained north of Memphis and Charleston Railroad, if possible; if not, to operate on Mississippi River below. Headquarters Chalmers' brigade always to be Oxford; Ferguson's, Verona or Okolona. A regiment for picket kept at Coldwater depot and crossing. Detached commands and new organizations to form at Panola. Kentucky Faulkner has 1,200 men (three regiments), one-third only armed and equipped. Forrest's force, fairly estimated, 3,000, inclusive of Faulkner. Logan's cavalry, of Jackson's division, to operate on the New Orleans and Jackson Railroad. A large side-wheeler, the Nashville, at Mobile; has engines in and is being plated; wheels protected by compressed cotton; will be the finest of the fleet when completed.

O.R.-- SERIES I--VOLUME XXXII/2 [S# 58]
UNION CORRESPONDENCE, ORDERS, AND RETURNS RELATING TO OPERATIONS IN KENTUCKY, SOUTHWEST VIRGINIA, TENNESSEE, MISSISSIPPI, ALABAMA, AND NORTH GEORGIA, FROM JANUARY 1, 1864, TO FEBRUARY 29, 1864.--#5

COLLINS DEPOT, *MISS.,*
January 15, 1864--2.30 *p.m.*
    Hon. A. LINCOLN,
    President United States:
DEAR SIR: I have but recently arrived from Central Mississippi (near Jackson), and send you this note to give you an item of information that may be of service to the country.
I learned from Maj. John S. Mellon, chief commissary at Grenada, Miss., that he was the author of the plan to burn all the steam-boats on the Mississippi River and its tributaries, and that his plan had been approved of by the authorities at Richmond. **There is a regularly organized band of boat-burners at Memphis, Saint Louis**, and other places. The plan of operations is to go on board the steamboats as deck-hands or passengers, and, as soon as opportunity affords, set fire to the boat and then escape. The boat being destroyed, the individual proceeds to Richmond and there receives his reward. I could give other information of the civil and military status of the South, but I forbear.

                                          S. W.
                                          SPEER.

OFFICIAL RECORDS OF THE UNION AND CONFEDERATE NAVIES IN THE WAR OF THE REBELLION, series 1, volume 26:

Report of Rear-Admiral Porter, U. S. Navy, transmitting captured letters referring to the institution of torpedo service.

MISSISSIPPI SQUADRON, FLAGSHIP BLACK HAWK,
Alexandria, La., March 20, 1864.

SIR: I have the honor to enclose you some rebel correspondence which was captured by the gunboat Signal a day or two since, while the rebel mail carrier was crossing the river. It gives a complete history of the rebel torpedoes, the machine that blew up the Housatonic, and the manner in which it was done. They have just appointed a torpedo corps (I send one of the commissions) for the purpose of blowing up property of all kinds. **Amongst other devilish inventions is a torpedo resembling a lump of coal, to be placed in coal piles and amongst the coal put on board vessels.** The names of the parties are all mentioned in the correspondence, and I send a photograph of one of them, which, if multiplied and put in the hands of detectives, may be of service.

I have given orders to commanders of vessels not to be very particular about the treatment of any of these desperadoes if caught only summary punishment will be effective. I trust that we will be prepared to avoid any of their machines.

I have the honor to be, very respectfully, your obedient servant,
DAVID D. PORTER,
Rear-Admiral.

Hon. GIDEON WELLES,
Secretary of the Navy, Washington, D. C.

[Enclosures.]
RICHMOND, VA., January 19, 1864.

MY DEAR COLONEL: I hope you have received all my letters. I wrote two to Mobile, one to Columbus, and two to Brandon, [Miss.]. I now send this by a party who is going to Shreveport and promised to learn your whereabouts, so as to forward it to you.

I have met with much delay and annoyance since you left. The castings have all been completed some time, and the coal is so perfect that the most critical eye could not detect it. The President thinks them perfect, but Mr. Seddon will do nothing without Congressional action, so I have been engaged for the last two weeks in getting up a bill that will cover my case; at last it has met his approval and will to-day go to the Senate, thence to the House in secret session. It provides that the Secretary of War shall have the power to organize a secret-service corps, commission, enlist, and detail parties, who shall retain former rank and pay; also give such compensation as he may deem fit, not exceeding 50 per cent, for property partially and totally destroyed; also to advance, when necessary, out of the secret-service fund, money to parties engaging to injure the enemy.

[portion deleted]

Your friend,

T. E. COURTENAY.

Colonel H. E. CLARK,
7th. Missouri Cavalry,
Major-General Price's Headquarters, Arkansas.
OFFICIAL RECORDS OF THE UNION AND CONFEDERATE
NAVIES IN THE WAR OF THE REBELLION, Series 1 Volume 27:

HEADQUARTERS DEPARTMENT OF THE MISSOURI,
Office of Provost-Marshal-General,
St. Louis, Mo., March 9, 1865.

ADMIRAL: Enclosed please find a copy of a letter written by Admiral
Porter to this office about one year ago, in which mention is made of a
certain letter, then in his possession, written by one T. E. Courtenay to
Colonel Clark, of the rebel Army, relative to the destruction of gunboats
and transports on the Mississippi River. This Courtenay is now under
arrest, and I respectfully request that you furnish this office with the
original letter addressed by Courtenay to Colonel Clark, as we have good
reason to believe that evidence sufficient to convict him can be obtained.
Very respectfully, your obedient servant,

J. H. BAKER,
Provost-Marshal-General, Department of the Missouri.

Rear-Admiral LEE,
Commanding Mississippi Squadron.

OFFICIAL RECORDS OF THE UNION AND CONFEDERATE
NAVIES IN THE WAR OF THE REBELLION, series 1, volume 26:

General order of Rear-Admiral Porter, U. S. Navy, urging vigilance
against destructive inventions of the enemy.

U.S. MISSISSIPPI SQUADRON, FLAGSHIP BLACK HAWK,
Alexandria, La., March 20, 1864.

GENERAL ORDER,}
No. 184.   }

**The enemy have adopted new inventions to destroy human life and
vessels in the shape of torpedoes, and an article resembling coal,
which is to be placed in our coal piles for the purpose of blowing the
vessels up,** or injuring them. Officers will have to be careful in overlook-

ing coal barges. Guards will be placed over them at all times, and anyone found attempting to place any of these things amongst the coal will be shot on the spot.

The same policy will be adopted toward those persons who are caught planting torpedoes, or floating them down, or with any of these inventions in their possession.

[portion deleted]

DAVID D. PORTER,
Rear-Admiral, Commanding Mississippi Squadron.

North & South Magazine Article

The article version of Sultana: A Case For Sabotage originally published in North & South Magazine, Volume 5, Number 1, December 2001 went through a number of versions and peer reviews before publication. The published version contained 61 endnotes, compared to the original 128, and was approximately half the length of the submitted article. As a number of people over the years have asked where to find the article, and North & South sadly went out business in 2013 after 16 years of publication, the originally published text is included here.

SULTANA: A Case For Sabotage

by D. H. Rule

"...the result of no accident, but of fiendish design."[1]

Seven miles out of Memphis, at 2:00 a.m. on April 27, 1865, the steamer *Sultana* chugged northward loaded with over twenty-three hundred people, most of them Union soldiers returning home from southern prison camps. Without warning, an explosion ripped through the boilers. Scalding steam burst out and a shower of flaming coal shot upward into the night, raining downward on the crowded boat. In moments the steamer was engulfed in flames. Over seventeen hundred people died, making the destruction of the *Sultana* a maritime disaster worse than the sinking of the *Titanic*.[2]

AT ANY OTHER TIME, the event would have raised an outcry, but it faded quickly into near obscurity, for the attention of both nations, Union and Confederate, was focused eastward—first on Lee's surrender in Virginia, then on the death of President Lincoln. Three investigations into the *Sultana* disaster followed. Only a brief time was spent in Memphis seeking the exact cause of the explosion, before the investigators moved on to concentrate on who was responsible for overloading the boat in Vicksburg. Though sabotage was not conclusively ruled out, neither was it strongly investigated. The destruction of the *Sultana* was eventually dismissed as the result of either a flaw in the boilers, a faulty boiler repair, or negligence in letting the water level fall too low in the boilers.

There the matter remained for twenty-three years. Then on May 6, 1888, an article appeared in the *St. Louis Globe-Democrat* citing a St. Louis resident named William C. Streetor who claimed that a "Confederate mail carrier and blockade runner" named "Robert Lowden," alias "Charles Dale," had actually destroyed the *Sultana* in an act of sabotage. "I had the statement from his own lips," Streetor told the newspaper.[3]

Two days later the *Memphis Daily Appeal* printed a substantially abbreviated version of the article on May 8, 1888, but it had little impact. Most historians have dismissed it as a mere footnote to the event. Typical is the comment of James W. Elliot in *Transport to Disaster* (1962) that "the idea [of sabotage] was adopted by the usual weird assortment of cranks and publicity seekers."[4]

The answers to the fate of the *Sultana* were not to be found in Memphis, where the tragedy occurred, nor in Vicksburg, where the original Federal investigations focused, but in St. Louis. There could be found two extremely significant items: the identities and histories of Streetor and Lowden.

The St. Louis resident who made the claim of Confederate sabotage against the *Sultana* was William C. Streetor, a local sign painter. Streetor had enlisted in the Union army in St. Louis in May of 1861.[5] Streetor was also the assistant keeper and chief clerk of Gratiot Street Prison, the Federal prison established in St. Louis in December 1861, working for the provost marshal's office.[6] The man Streetor claimed confessed to blowing up the *Sultana* was Robert Louden (note spelling), a Confederate agent who smuggled mail and was notorious for the destruction of steamboats along the Mississippi River. "There is not another man in this or any other state as dangerous a spy as this R. Louden," said St. Louis Provost Marshal George E. Leighton in 1863. After the war Louden was partners in a painting business with William C. Streetor. If anyone was in a position to know Louden's secrets, it was Streetor.[7]

ROBERT LOUDEN was the eldest son of Scottish immigrants Andrew Louden, a carpenter, and his wife Cecelia.[8] Robert was a native of Philadelphia, Pennsylvania, where as a young man, he worked as a painter. Around 1850 he killed a man in Philadelphia. He fled to St. Louis where he was traced, arrested, and returned to Philadelphia for trial. Louden was convicted of manslaughter and sent to Eastern State Penitentiary on December 3, 1852.[9]

Prisoners at Eastern State Penitentiary were totally isolated from all human contact on the theory that they would reflect their crimes and become penitent. In fact the solitary confinement came to be known as a "maniac maker," with a disproportionately high rate of insanity among the prisoners, some of whom were pardoned as their mental conditions deteriorated. Charles Dickens, in *American Notes*, said of Eastern State, "It is my fixed opinion that those who have undergone this punishment MUST pass into society again morally unhealthy and diseased.... What monstrous phantoms, bred of despondency and doubt, and born and reared in solitude, have stalked upon the earth, making creation ugly, and darkening the face of Heaven![10] Robert Louden was pardoned on May 19, 1854, a year before the expiration of his sentence; prison records are silent as to the reason.

Louden left Philadelphia and returned to St. Louis using the name "Charles Deal." As Deal, Louden joined the Liberty Fire Company No. 6, one of the combative, competitive volunteer fire companies in 1850's St. Louis. His younger brother James also joined the company, under the alias James Deal. A historian of the volunteer fire companies said of the Liberty, "they acquired unfortunately more of the Eastern rowdies than all the rest [of the fire companies] combined." The volunteer fire companies were abolished in 1858 in favor of professional organizations, and the Liberty Fire House was burned on February 11, 1858, by, it was said, "some of the disaffected members."[11]

Before its demise, the volunteer fire department gave Louden valuable social, political, and business connections in the city. One prominent member of Liberty was John M. Wimer, mayor of St. Louis. In 1860 Wimer's business partner was a man named Thomas E. Courtenay, who was sheriff of St. Louis County in 1860. Courtenay would later play a key role in the sabotage of Mississippi steamboats.[12]

On August 31, 1858, using his correct name, Louden married Mary J. Gibson. She was the sister of Louisa Gibson McCoy, wife of Arthur C. McCoy, another member of the Liberty Fire Company. McCoy became a Confederate captain, scout, and spy under General Joseph Shelby. Louden's new wife, Mary Gibson, was a young widow with two daughters by her late first husband, William L. Lynch. When Robert Louden wed Mary Gibson he married into one of the oldest families in Missouri. His mother-in-law, Heloise Daguet Gibson, was descended from some of the earliest French settlers in Ste. Genevieve. His father-in-law, William Gibson, was closely related to the Dent family—the in-laws of Ulysses S. Grant. Soon after his marriage into this well-to-do family, Louden went into business for himself, painting houses, signs, and—significantly—steamboats. By the outbreak of the war the couple had a daughter of their own.[13]

St. Louis in early 1861 was a city of divided loyalties. Though an eastern northerner by upbringing, Robert Louden chose the southern cause, joining the pro-secession Minute Men.[14] Two of Robert Louden's brothers, James and Andrew, also went with the Confederacy, while their sister's husband joined the Union army. New York-born William Streetor, also a painter who may have already worked with Louden, chose the Union side, joining the 3rd Missouri Reserve Corp., USA, in response to Frank Blair's call.

A report by a Union spy claimed that Robert Louden and Arthur McCoy were dangerous men and "the head and front of all mischief, and that they planned to kill congressman Frank Blair.[15] Robert Louden again came to Union officials' attention on June 30, 1862, when he was charged with "giving expression to treasonable sentiments." No action was taken on the charge. Little did the officials know that Louden was already an active Confederate courier and mail carrier. It is possible he was already responsible for the burning of Mississippi River steamboats.[16]

Earlier that year Louden had met the "Official Confederate Mail Carrier" for General Sterling Price's army, Absalom C. Grimes. Before the war Grimes had been a steamboat pilot on the upper Mississippi River. He had been relatively neutral until John B. Gray tried to force Grimes and several other steamer pilots (including Sam Bowen and Samuel Clemens—later Mark Twain) into service ferrying troops on the Missouri River. Grimes then joined the Southern cause with enthusiasm, causing a breach in his own family as a younger brother joined the Union army. After a stint as a private in the cavalry, during which he was captured and escaped twice, Grimes decided to carry letters from Missouri families with him as he went south to rejoin his unit. The letters were so gratefully received that Grimes was commissioned as a major on detached secret service duty, assigned as an official mail carrier by General Sterling Price.[17]

Robert Louden and Absalom Grimes became partners in the mail carrying business, both passing through the lines numerous times, moving about freely within Union territory. While carrying mail between families and lonely soldiers may seem a harmless enough enterprise, Union authorities had early on declared mail carrying between the lines to be the equivalent of spying, and punishable by death. Captured letters were a tremendous prize for the wealth of information about Confederate sympathizers, and troop strengths and movements they contained; waves of arrests in St. Louis followed closely after the capture of any Rebel mail.[18] Both Louden and Grimes also carried official Confederate dispatches to other agents who worked behind the lines, and to secret Rebel organizations. Louden seems to have been one of the primary couriers between General Price and northern Copperhead organizations. Grimes, in his memoirs, praised Louden's unlimited courage and good judgment," and referred to Louden "amusing himself burning government steamboats." Louden's employment as a fireman certainly gave him the knowledge of how to make things burn effectively. His experience painting steamboats also taught him about their operations and their vulnerabilities.[19]

According to Grimes, by the summer of 1862 Federal authorities had become aware of the existence of a regular mail service between the Rebels in Missouri and the Confederate army. Peter Tallon—who became chief of U.S. Police in St. Louis in 1863—described a July 1862 encounter with Louden. The two went from saloon to saloon together while Louden delivered letters from the southern army. On August 11, 1862, Louden was arrested in a St. Louis saloon with about one hundred letters in his possession, and taken to Gratiot Street Prison. There to receive him was the assistant keeper of the prison, William C. Streetor.[20]

Charged with mail carrying, and being in the Rebel army and within Union lines without permission, Louden was sentenced to imprisonment for the duration of the war and transferred to Alton Prison twenty-five miles away in Illinois on August 20, but he jumped overboard and escaped.[21] Soon after, on September 2, Grimes was arrested in St. Louis in possession of a large southbound mail. He was tried on charges of being a mail carrier and spy and sentenced to be shot. Though held in close confinement, chained and heavily guarded, Grimes again demonstrated his talent for escaping a month later.

Louden and Grimes had both received a clear taste of the perils of their professions, but this did not cause them to slacken their mail smuggling and courier activities. Grimes said of Louden that "the sideline of steamboat burning was accredited to him and he was, therefore, much in demand by the Federals." A Federal report at the end of November 1862 noted that twenty steamers had been destroyed within the previous two months. Some of these may have been the work of Robert Louden; according to Streetor, "he told me he had fired no less than half a dozen steamboats on the Mississippi."[22]

On December 3, 1862, Robert Louden's stepdaughter, Mary Lynch, died in St. Louis and was buried in Calvary Cemetery near Robert's brother James, who had died in March. Robert Louden, wanted by Federal authorities, probably could not attend her burial.[23] Efforts to find Louden now reached a new level. On April 25, Louden's wife was arrested and taken to Gratiot Street Prison, where she was pressured to reveal her husband's location. The cell in which she was kept had been used for dissections when the building was a medical college, and the floors were stained with blood. When the floors above were washed, water ran down through the ceiling, drenching her.[24] One of her jailers taunted her about the recent death of her daughter, and Mary—already desperately ill—fell into a coughing fit that left her choking on her own blood, yet medical care was denied her.

Eight days after Mary's imprisonment, Louden's father was arrested in Philadelphia, and taken to Fort McHenry, Maryland. A Rebel mail had been delivered in Philadelphia and suspicion fell on Andrew Louden. It was soon learned, however, that it was his son, Robert, who was responsible. "The military authorities of St. Louis are very desirous of catching young Loudon as they wish to try him as a spy and hang him," wrote Lieutenant Colonel William Whipple, who had ordered the father's arrest.[25] Instead of being released, Andrew Louden was banished to the South, never having been convicted of any crime. His family apparently believed he had been killed.

On May 13, 1863 Robert's wife, along with two dozen other St. Louis civilians, half of them women, were banished. Mary Louden was forced to leave her young daughters behind, and with the others was put on board a steamer and sent down river to Memphis. One of the banished women in later years recalled the name of the steamer that carried them into exile as the *Sultana*, but several St. Louis newspapers gave the name as the *Belle Memphis*. It is possible that this episode may have given Louden a personal motive to target the *Sultana* when the opportunity arose. The two boats, sidewheelers of virtually the same size, were easily confused, and both had been at Memphis at about this time. The captain of the *Belle Memphis* in May 1863 was a man named James Cass Mason, and he was destined, on April 27, 1865, to be the captain of the *Sultana*.[26]

After his wife's expulsion Louden continued his clandestine activities with a passion. In June he and Grimes ran mail through the blockade of Vicksburg. After the city's surrender, Louden joined Grimes on the Confederate steamer *Prince of Wales*, but this was burned shortly thereafter to keep it from falling into Union hands. On July 14 Grimes, probably accompanied by Louden, assisted Commander Isaac N. Brown of the Confederate navy in placing torpedoes that destroyed the Union gunboat *De Kalb*.[27]

It was at this time that Federal officials began to refer to Louden and others as the "organized boat-burners." Though apparently organized earlier, it was only now that the saboteurs began soliciting the Confederate government for financial support based on the value of Federal property destroyed. Joseph W. Tucker, St. Louis newspaper editor and Southern Methodist minister, was the leader of the organized boat-burners under General Price and his adjutant Colonel Thomas L. Snead. During the siege of Vicksburg Tucker solicited $20,000 from General Joseph E. Johnston to support the boat-burning effort, and continued to lobby Richmond for financial support for the rest of the war.[28] Other members of the organized boat-burners included

John Richard Barret, former Missouri congressman from St. Louis, believed by the Federals to have been head of land operations; Thomas L. Clark, a saloon keeper from Grenada, Mississippi; Minor Majors, second in command under Tucker; and Robert Louden. The organized boat-burners reported their strikes to Richmond through Tucker, after which payment was dispensed.[29]

The destruction of the steamer *Ruth* can undoubtedly be credited to Robert Louden. Shortly before midnight on the night of August 4, after a refueling stop at Cairo, Illinois, the *Ruth* caught fire. The boat was en route to Vicksburg with eight Union paymasters and $2.6 million dollars in army payroll. The money was reported destroyed, and twenty-six of the one hundred fifty passengers, military and civilian, were killed. Grimes, in his memoirs, places the blame squarely on Robert Louden. St. Louis provost marshal documents also link Louden to the burning of the *Ruth*.[30]

On September 3 Louden's boat-burning career was rudely interrupted when he was arrested in St. Louis. The St. Louis newspapers reported Louden's arrest with gleeful detail. The house in which he was sleeping was surrounded by a squad of cavalry while four U. S. Police officers went in and secured wanted man. After they declined to accept his word of honor not to escape if they did not handcuff him, Louden managed to talk the four police officers into stopping at a saloon for a drink en route to the prison. After downing his liquor, Louden bolted for the door. He was caught and taken to Myrtle Street Prison where, amidst a great deal of "splenetic abuse" aimed at his captors, Louden promised that when he escaped he would "patch his pants with the scalps of Federal soldiers." Louden was "substantially licked" in the one-sided fight that followed.

In Louden's possession at the time of his arrest was a note, in his own hand, dated September 2, 1863 saying, "...I believe we will make a great stroke tonight... everything depends on speed & courage we will have a glorious success or a glorious death. "The note was signed "R. L.," with the added initials OAK nearby. OAK were the initials of the Order of American Knights, a secret organization committed to waging the war behind Union lines. Though the Order claimed a huge membership, and promised grand actions, relatively few key individuals played any real role. In St. Louis, OAK was connected to the organized boat-burners, who in turn were connected to, and part of, the Confederate secret service operations. The military head of OAK was General Sterling Price, Louden's commander.[31]

Louden's arrest on the third of September did not prevent this comrades from carrying out his "great stroke" on the thirteenth, when they burned the *Imperial, Jesse K. Bell, Hiawatha, Post Boy*, and a barge loaded with freight at the foot of Market Street in St. Louis, vessels valued at about a quarter of a million dollars. These were major losses.[32]

[sidebar]
THE PAYMASTERS
In April 1865 Edward Frazor, one of the imprisoned boat-burners, made a confession in which he referred he and others had made to Richmond in the summer of 1864 (*OR*, Series I, Volume 48, Pt. 2, p. 194):

"At Richmond, Clark introduced me to the Secretary of War, Secretary Seddon, Clark told his business, when he sent us to the Secretary of State, J.P. Benjamin. I believe he looked our statement over and took time to consider.... The next day I went there, and Mr. Benjamin asked me if I knew all these claims for destroying U.S. property were right and correct. I told him they were, as far as I knew. He then offered $30,000 in green-backs to settle. I told him I could not take that. Then he said he would take time to study again....

"Benjamin next offered $35,000 in gold. Then Clark went to see him, and before he went I told him to get all be could, but not take less than the $35,000 down and get all the more he could. When he came back he said he had taken the $35,000 down and $15,000 on deposit, payable in four months from date, provided those claims of the Louisville matter (burning of Government medical stores last year) were all right. I think that is the way the receipt read. I went over to Benjamin's to sign the receipt, and while I was there the President, Jefferson Davis, sent for me. I went in to see

him with Mr. Benjamin. Mr. Davis was talking about sending men up here to destroy the long bridge, near Nashville.
He asked me if I knew anything about it—knew where it was.
I told him I did. He asked me which would be the best route
to send men up here to do it. I told him I thought it was
rather dangerous to send men up here who had never been
here. He wanted to know if I would not take charge of it. I
told [him] yes, provided he would stop all men from coming
up here, as they would only hinder the work. He said he
would do it, and wanted to know if I wanted any men from
there to help me. I said I didn't. Benjamin said the pay
would be $400,000 for burning the bridge. After we got all
ready to leave Mr. Benjamin gave us a draft for $34,800 in
gold on Columbia, S.C. ... Clark got passes from the Secretary of War, twelve or thirteen in all."
[end sidebar]

Louden was held for three weeks in Myrtle Street Prison,
then moved to Gratiot Street Prison, where he was put in the
same cell in which his wife had been kept. A ball and chain
were attached to his leg and he was held in close confinement, allowed contact with no one. In a strange letter to his
brother Andrew (2nd Lieutenant, 16th Mississippi Infantry,
wounded and captured at Gettysburg, a POW at Johnson's
Island, Ohio) dated November 1,[33] Robert writes that he was
in St. Louis only to take his daughters to a convent, and
mentions Mary, her banishment, and how he hadn't seen her
but once.[34] He also discusses the cruel and inhuman way the
Federals treated his father, and that his mother "was about
frantic at his loss and the way they murdered him." He then
alludes to taking revenge. The letter seems to have been
aimed at the provost marshal officials who would read it
first, rather than at his brother. Louden's father returned to
Philadelphia from the South four days after this letter was
written, so Louden may not have known he was alive.[35]

Louden was tried in December on charges of being a mail
carrier, spy, and boat-burner. He was found guilty on all
charges and sentenced to be hanged. His mail-running
partner, Absalom Grimes, had been arrested in Memphis in

November and returned to St. Louis where he was also tried and sentenced to death.[36]

As the date of his execution neared, Louden wrote a letter pleading for clemency. He confessed his guilt to all charges, including boat-burning, saying, "I am deeply and truly penitent for all I have done and pray for forgiveness." After talking about the plight of his "afflicted wife and helpless family," he ends by "solemnly pledging never again to transgress the laws of my country." Of course, to Louden "my country" was the C.S.A., not the U.S.A.! Streetor later called Louden, "cool and calculating in his disposition."[37]

A last-minute reprieve arrived on May 6, 1864, only hours before Louden was to be hanged, a reprieve Grimes claimed was due to the intervention of a St. Louis priest and a nun. However, Louden's mother had rushed to Washington, D.C. to plead with the president for clemency when she learned of her son's impending execution. A telegram dated May 5th from the president's office, enquiring if the execution date had been set, suggests her interview with Lincoln may have saved her son's life.[38]

But it was only a reprieve. The death sentence hung over Louden during the summer of 1864 as the St. Louis Order of American Knights leaders—Dunn, Hunt, and others—were arrested and confessed the secrets of their organization.[39]

In June, with his execution date nearing, Grimes led a desperate escape attempt in which several men were killed. Grimes was shot and it was thought for a time that he would die. Louden was involved in the escape attempt but failed to get away. Among those who did so were Jasper C. Hill and William H. Sebring, both of whom made their way to Canada where they joined Thomas H. Hines, Bennett H. Young, John B. Castleman, and other Confederate agents.[40]

On October 3, with the Federals believing General Price was threatening the security of St. Louis prisons, Louden and a number of other prisoners from Gratiot were transferred to Alton Prison a short distance up the river in Illinois. Grimes, still recovering in the prison hospital, managed to smuggle a file to Louden. While on the steamer to Alton, Louden filed through the chain that handcuffed him to another prisoner, slipped over the side of the boat, and escaped.[41] Advisories were widely circulated with Louden's description. Everyone who may have had any connection to Louden's escape, except Grimes, was questioned vigorously, but he was not found.[42]

Louden's wife, who had been allowed to return to the North after his arrest, had gone with the children to Philadelphia to stay with his family. A telegram was sent from St. Louis to Philadelphia instructing authorities there to arrest Mary Louden and Robert's father, and to hold them as "hostages" in case Louden attempted to go there.[43]

For several months there was no word of Louden. Grimes later said Louden that had successfully made his escape to the South. Streetor confirms, he "made his way South, where he remained until after the close of the war." J. H. Baker, provost marshal general of the Department of the Missouri, continued to investigate the boat-burners. William Murphy of New Orleans turned himself in and named his comrades, then vanished. In February Baker arrested, among several others, Edward Frazor, a steamboat striker from St. Louis, who made full confession, naming the other boat-burners and detailing their connection to the Confederate government. Robert Louden's name was prominent on a list headed by Tucker, Majors, and Barret.[44]

In March the hunt for Louden intensified . Advisories with his description and orders to arrest him were sent from St. Louis to a number of other cities. Provost Marshal Baker believed that Louden had been arrested in New Orleans, though authorities there claimed Louden had never been in their custody. Several of the officers in New Orleans knew Louden and had a photograph of him and the city was searched thoroughly.[45]

At this time Louden's former smuggling partner, Absalom Grimes, made a trip to New Orleans. Grimes had been granted a full pardon by President Lincoln on December 10, 1864, owing to the influence of several of his Union steamboat colleagues and friends. Grimes married his fiancée, Lucy Glascock of Ralls County, Missouri, on March 7, 1865 and a short time thereafter took a honeymoon trip to New

Orleans on the steamer *Henry Von Phul*. The pilot of the *Von Phul* was Sam Bowen, a friend of Grimes who had aided the smuggling efforts throughout the war. It is curious that Grimes should choose to go to New Orleans at this time for he was a known Confederate agent who had been actively sought up and down the river. Two weeks after being pardoned he was in fact arrested by the sheriff in Hannibal, Missouri, who hadn't heard of his release. He also had a close call with some Federal soldiers seeking to lynch him. For the erstwhile mail runner the Mississippi River was far from safe; not only was it still a war zone, but there were Federal officials at every Union-held town along the way, many of whom did not know of his pardon. Though Grimes casually describes the trip in his memoirs as "all sunshine," it was an enormously risky thing for a person in his position to undertake for anything less than an important cause.[46]

If, as Baker believed, Louden was in New Orleans in late March, and being actively sought, Grimes arrival in a steamer with a sympathetic pilot provided the perfect opportunity to leave the city. Furthermore, the boat would be returning upriver to Memphis, where Louden had numerous reliable associates. Not least among those in the area of Memphis at this time was Arthur C. McCoy, Louden's brother-in-law. Commanding a small band of Shelby's men set to watch the river and do what damage they could, McCoy was also sending spies into and out of Memphis, and Louden could certainly count on McCoy for support.[47]

Grimes and his new wife arrived back in St. Louis the day Lincoln died. Though Grimes gives details of Louden's escape in October 1864, his memoirs are strangely quiet about the latter's activities in 1865. With a pardon dated December 1864, Grimes had good cause to keep quiet about any association with Louden after that date.

In April 1865, just days before the *Sultana* arrived in Memphis, letters were being sent out from the St. Louis provost marshal's office naming nineteen men to whom Baker attributed the destruction of sixty boats. Louden was named as one of four men the authorities were most anxious to apprehend, the others being Tucker, Barret, and Isaac

Elshire. Elshire was credited with the destruction of the steamer *Robert Campbell, Jr.* on September 28, 1863. In an ironic twist, one of those killed in the destruction of the *Campbell* was David Lynch, former brother-in-law of Mary Louden.[48]

The *Sultana* arrived in Memphis near sunset on the evening of April 26. At 11:00 p.m. the boat moved across the river to take on coal. There she remained for two hours, leaving at 1:00 a.m. to head upriver, bearing over two thousand liberated prisoners, for whom the war was over, towards their northern homes.

At two o'clock in the morning, about seven miles north of Memphis, an explosion burst through the boat. Over seventeen hundred people died; burned, scalded, and drowned. As many Union soldiers were killed that night on the river as died on the battlefields of Shiloh.[49]

A MONTH AFTER THE DESTRUCTION of the *Sultana* the Confederate troops of the Department of the Trans-Mississippi surrendered, ending the war in the West. Many of the Missouri Confederate leaders fled to Mexico. The investigation of the boat-burners was shifted to Washington, and Allen Pinkerton began tracking them. One of his reports placed Robert Louden in the Memphis area around the time of the destruction of the *Sultana*.[50]

William C. Streetor returned to his career as a painter, and raised an ever-growing family. Absalom Grimes resumed piloting steamboats. But by 1866, Robert Louden was dead—dead as far as St. Louis was concerned, that is, with his wife listed as a widow in the city directory. Living nearby, apparently fulfilling a promise he had made to take care of Mary and the children when Louden's execution was expected, was younger brother Andrew. "If it had come to the worst, Mary and them would never have wanted for anything while I lived," he had said.[51]

But by the spring of 1867 Robert Louden was back, alive and well, engaged in a painting business with William H. Gray. "His friends obtained a pardon for him from President Johnson," according to Streetor, "and, armed with that, he

returned to his home in St. Louis."[52] Less than two years
after the war had ended the ex-Confederate agent and the
ex-Union prison keeper were working together in the same
shop on Locust Street in St. Louis.[53]

THE WAR PASSED INTO HISTORY and the
memory of the *Sultana* tragedy faded. But the survivors
remembered. And so did William C. Streetor. The survivors
began to meet in 1885, to renew acquaintance and exchange
reminiscences. And in 1888 a startling tale emerged. After
the publication of the statements of some of the survivors in
the *St. Louis Globe-Democrat*, a reporter for the paper
interviewed William C. Streetor. "I can give the cause of the
explosion," Streetor said. "A torpedo inclosed in a lump of
coal was carried aboard the steamer at Memphis and deposited in the coal pile in front of the boilers for the express
purpose of causing her destruction."[54]

The method Streetor said Louden claimed to have used
was a bomb made to resemble a lump of coal, a type of bomb
known as a Courtenay Torpedo, named for its inventor,
Thomas E. Courtenay, former sheriff of St. Louis county. We
do know that only an hour before the explosion the *Sultana*
had taken on coal. Louden had the perfect opportunity,
under the cover of darkness and in the confusion of crowds
of people, to place his bomb. He was experienced with such
actions. "It had got to be too *** ticklish a job to set a boat
afire and get away from her," Louden is quoted as saying,
explaining why he had used a bomb.[55]

[sidebar]
THE BOMB
In March 1864, David D. Porter, Rear-Admiral Commanding Mississippi Squadron, issued General Order 184
which began, "The enemy have adopted new inventions to
destroy human life and vessels in the shape of torpedoes,
and an article resembling coal, which is to be placed in our
coal piles for the purpose of blowing the vessels up...." The
reference was to the type of bomb Louden claimed he used

to destroy the *Sultana*, known then as the "Courtenay Torpedo."

A Courtenay Torpedo was described by Lieutenant Barnes in *Submarine Warfare* as appearing to be an "innocent lump of coal, but is a block of cast-iron with a core containing about ten pounds of powder." The device was covered with tar and coal powder, making it indistinguishable from the rest of the coal. J. Thomas Scharf in *History of the Confederate States Navy* says that when the Courtenay Torpedoes were taken aboard Federal boats with the coal they "exploded with terrible effect [to] their boilers." A *New York Times* article of May 18, 1865 said, "This was the awful contrivance employed with so much success by the rebels in blowing up our transports on the Mississippi, and it is suspected that the awful disaster to the *Sultana* as accomplished by one of these diabolical things."[56]
[end sidebar]

Several of the statements made by witnesses of the disaster at the time lend credence to Louden's story. William Rowberry—the first mate of the *Sultana*—blamed sabotage, claiming the boat was running well until the moment of the blast. The theory of a shell exploding in the furnace was "actively discussed and [had] many believers among experienced river men."[57] More compelling are the descriptions of the explosion itself. A newspaper reported a witness seeing the furnace door blow open before the boilers burst. Survivors mentioned flaming coals flying about. George Byron Merrick in *Old Times on the Upper Mississippi*, in the chapter entitled "Killing Steamboats," describes how even a little explosion in the furnaces would throw "live coals over the deck." Witnesses describing the 1858 destruction of the steamer *Pennsylvania*, however, in which four boilers exploded, make no mention of coals or burning wood from the furnace flying about, and say it took over half an hour before the boat took fire.[58]

Robert Louden was certainly capable of sabotaging the *Sultana*. He had already demonstrated his willingness, and ability, to sneak aboard boats and destroy them, without

regard to lives lost. Louden was a calm, professional saboteur unafraid of taking risks. "He possessed bravery of a
certain kind, I think, equal to that of any man who ever
lived," said Streetor.[59] In late April 1865 no payments from
Richmond could be expected, yet the *Sultana* was selected
for destruction. On the Mississippi saboteurs could not
simply place their torpedoes randomly, as they might in
some eastern areas, because many of the steamer pilots and
crews were sympathetic to the South and engaged in smuggling for the Confederacy throughout the war. *Sultana* might
have been a target of opportunity, but it was nevertheless
deliberately targeted.

Would Louden have fabricated the tale he told to
Streetor? It seems unlikely. William C. Streetor—a loyal
Union man, a St. Louis businessman, and respected member
of the Grand Army of the Republic—certainly believed it. As
Streetor recalled:

At times he [Louden] drank heavily, and when in his cups
was disposed to talk a little too much for a man with a record
like he had. It was while talking about the war, and the
burning of so many boats by the Confederate agents came up
in the course of the conversation. He told me that he had
fired no less than half a dozen steamboats on the Mississippi. I asked him in an offhand way what he knew about the
Sultana explosion. Then he told me the story of the torpedo
in the coal....[60]

As for Robert Louden, he had an abundance of stories
about his exploits during the war sufficient to last a lifetime.
He had no reason to make up others, especially a story that
could bring the personal vengeance of survivors down onto
him. Louden left St. Louis shortly after his drunken confession to Streetor, and reportedly died of yellow fever in New
Orleans in September of the same year.[61]

Was Robert Louden responsible for the destruction of the
Sultana? We will probably never know for sure. What we do
know is that he was a convicted killer who joined the Liberty
Fire Company under an alias; that he was a member of the
"organized boat-burners" who were responsible for the

destruction of at least sixty Mississippi steamboats; that he was responsible for the destruction of the steamboat *Ruth*; that when captured he threatened to "patch his pants with the scalps of Federal soldiers": that there is evidence that he was in the area at the time; *and that he claimed he had carried a bomb onboard the SULTANA in order to effect her destruction.*

Though dismissed by investigators at the time, and by historians since, the possibility that the *Sultana* was destroyed by Robert Louden is deserving of much more serious consideration than it has yet received.

Article Endnotes:

[1] *St. Louis Globe-Democrat*, May 6, 1888.

[2] Potter, Jerry O., *The Sultana Tragedy: America's Greatest Maritime Disaster* (Pelican Publishing Company, Inc.: 1992).

[3] National Archives and Records Administration (hereafter NARA), Record Group (RG) 153, unnumbered microfilm series, Washburn Commission Records, Dana Commission Records, Hoffman Investigation Records.

[4] Most *Sultana* historians to date have cited the abbreviated *Memphis Daily Appeal* article, as the search for information about the disaster has, naturally, centered around Memphis. In the Memphis article, Streetor's name is misspelled "Streeter"; Elliot, James W., *Transport to Disaster* (Holt, Rinehart and Winston: 1962), p. 212.

[5] NARA, RG 94, M405, roll 402, Compiled Service Records, 3rd US Res. Corp.

[6] NARA, RG 109, M416, rolls 9092, Union Provost Marshal's Files of Papers Relating to Two or More Civilians, payroll records in George E. Leighton Collection , Missouri Historical Society.

[7] NARA, RG 109, M345, roll 170, Union Provost Marshal's Files of Papers Relating to Individual Civilians; Grimes, Absalom C., *Confederate Mail Runner*, edited by M.M. Quaife (ed.) (New Haven, Connecticut: 1926); *St. Louis Globe-Democrat*, May 6, 1888.

⁸ Her name is listed as Cecelia in the 1850 census but as Christina in an 1890 Philadelphia business directory.

⁹ 1850 US Census, Pennsylvania, Philadelphia County, Spruce Ward, 347; Pennsylvania State Archives, Eastern State Penitentiary Administration Records, RG 15, Descriptive Registers 63946, Admission and Discharge Registers 61814 ;NARA RG 94, M797, roll 40; Case File Investigations by Levi C. Turner and Lafayette C. Baker 1861-1866, report 1226 on Robert Louden by Chief of Police of Philadelphia, Benjamin Franklin.

¹⁰ Charles Dickens, *American Notes for General Circulation* (1842).

¹¹ Thomas Lynch, *Volunteer Fire Department of St. Louis*, 1880 (Missouri Historical Society).

¹² John M. Wimer was mayor in 1860. He died in battle in 1863 as a Confederate Colonel. Wimer and Courtenay were real estate and general agents in business together (Edwards *1860 St. Louis City Directory*).

¹³ Arthur C. McCoy was one of founders of the Minute Men who, with Basil Duke, Colton Greene, J. Rock Champion, and James Quinlan, raised a Missouri state flag over the St. Louis Courthouse in March 1861. The secessionist flag they flew over the Minute Men headquarters was said to have been sewn by Louisa Gibson McCoy (*Reminiscences of Basil Duke*, by General Basil Duke, 1911). After the war McCoy was alleged to have been involved in several bank and train robberies with the James-Younger gang; *1859 St. Louis Directory*.

¹⁴ Records of Louden's official military career are sketchy. He was in the Minute Men, an early Missouri State Guard unit. Louden and McCoy had been captured at Camp Jackson and exchanged: M.M.C. Hopewell, *Camp Jackson: History of the Missouri Volunteer Militia of St. Louis*, 1861, Independence, Missouri, 1997). An 1863 Federal report says he was a Confederate captain under General Price. Grimes' daughter, in a postwar magazine article, claims Louden had been a major; NARA, RG 94, M797 roll 405, roll 402. A Louden appears on a roster of Company D. McLaren Guards M.E.F Pollock Papers, Record of Camp Jackson Parolees Exchanged for Federal Prisoners After the Battle of Lexington, Missouri Historical Society; NARA RG 94, M797 roll

40. "The Blockade Runners of Vicksburg" by Mrs. Charlotte Grimes Mitchell, *Valley Trust Magazine*, Volume 6, Number 1, July, 1928.

[15] NARA, RG 109, M345, roll 170, letter by George E. Leighton; Broadhead Papers, 1861 spy report to the Union Safety Committee, Missouri Historical Society; NARA, RG 109, M345, roll 170, letter by George E. Leighton; NARA RG 109, M269 roll 244, service records of Andrew Louden.

[16] NARA, RG 109, M345, roll 170. At least one contemporary suggests that Louden was already an active boat-burner at this time.

[17] Grimes, 4; NARA, RG 109, M322 roll 4, Compiled Service Records, 1st Mo. Cav. CSA, letter by Mrs. Charlotte Grimes to Provost Marshal requesting permission to visit her son; Enlistment records Charles F. Grimes, Co. H, 142nd Inf. Reg. IL, Co. I, 149th Inf. Reg. IL, service records of Absalom C. Grimes; in Federal records Grimes is often referred to as "The Rebel Mail Carrier."

[18] *Official Records Of The Union And Confederate Navies In The War Of The Rebellion* (hereafter *ORN*), Series 1 Volume 24, page 427; The patterns of arrests following captured mails in St. Louis can also be seen in the Gratiot Street Prison ledgers; NARA RG109, M598, roll 72 and Provost Marshal files NARA RG 109, M416, rolls 9092, as well as blunt statements in St. Louis newspapers saying stories of captured mail had been withheld until arrests had been made.

[19] NARA RG 109, M345, roll 170,171 / RG 94, M797, roll 40; Grimes, 63.

[20] NARA, RG 109, M345, roll 170, report of Capt. Peter Tallon dated October 1863 referring to incidents of July 1862; George E. Leighton Papers, Provost Marshal payroll records, Missouri Historical Society.

[21] NARA, RG 109, M345, roll 170; *St. Louis Democrat*, September 4, 1863.

[22] Grimes, 67 ; *ORN*, Series 1 Volume 23, Page 511, letter by Lewis B. Parsons, Colonel and Assistant Quartermaster; *St. Louis Globe-Democrat*, May 6, 1888.

[23] Calvary Cemetery burial records; St. Louis city death records.

24 NARA, RG 109, M598 rolls 72, 145, Gratiot prison ledgers ; NARA, RG 109, M345, roll 170; Missouri Division of the United Daughters of the Confederacy *Reminiscences of the Women of Missouri During the Sixties,* "Reminiscences of Mrs. Lucy Nick-olson Lindsay," reprinted Dayton, Ohio, 1988. Supporting evidence of the conditions in Gratiot Street Prison at this time are found in Federal inspection reports: *War Of The Rebellion: A Compilation of the Official Records of the Union and Confederate Armies,* 128 volumes, hereafter OR (*Washington, DC: 1880-1906*), Series II, Volume 6, page 150.

25 NARA, RG 109, M345, roll 170.

26 Several of the banished women were part of Grimes' and Louden's mail smuggling operation; *Rem. Women,* "History of Events Preceding and Following the Banishment of Mrs. Margaret A. McLure, as Given to the Author by Herself." Winter, William C., The Civil War in St. Louis: A Guided Tour (St. Louis, Missouri: 1994), citing *Missouri Republican,* May 14, 1863, and *Missouri Democrat,* May 14, 1863; *OR,* Series I, Volume 23, Pt. 2, p. 323.

27 *ORN,* Series I, Volume 25, pp. 283-86, 290; *OR,* Series I, Volume 28, Pt. 2, p. 195; The Charles Parsons Papers, Missouri Historical Society.

28 Galusha Anderson in *Story of a Border City During the War* (1908), says Tucker was a Presbyterian minister. Reynolds, Thom-as C. (Confederate governor-in-exile of Missouri) "General Sterling Price and the Confederacy," unpublished manuscript, Missouri Historical Society; *OR,* Series I, Volume 24, Pt. 3, p. 1066; Tidwell, William A., with James O. Hall and David Winfred Gaddy, *Come Retribution* (Jackson, Mississippi 1988); *OR,* Series IV, Volume 3, pp. 125, 239; Letter from Tucker to Jefferson Davis, Jeff. Davis, "Constitutionalist."

29 Parsons Papers.

30 Ronald Horstman, "The Loss of the Government Greenbacks on the Steamer *Ruth," Missouri Historical Review,* Volume 70, No. 2, January 1972; *OR,* Series I, Volume 24, Pt. 3, p. 580; *OR,* Series III, Volume 3, p. 985; Grimes, 105; NARA, RG 109, M345, roll 170, report to President Lincoln of the case against Robert Louden.

[31] *Missouri Republican* and *St. Louis Democrat*, September 4, 1863; NARA, RG 109, M345, roll 170; General Sterling Price was military head of the OAK (Castel, Albert, *General Sterling Price and the Civil War in the West*, Baton Rouge, Louisiana: 1968); *OR*, Series I, Volume 7, pp. 231, 232). Price also authorized the boat-burners under Tucker, and a secret service corps under Thomas Courtenay, (*OR*, Series I, Volume 22, Pt. 2, p. 970; *OR*, Series IV, Volume 3, p. 202; Series II, Volume 8, p. 516). There are numerous other sources documenting the connections.

[32] *Encyclopedia of the History of St. Louis*, edited by William Hyde and Howard L. Conard (The Southern History Company: 1899).

[33] NARA, RG 109 , M269, roll 244, Compiled Service Records of Confederate Soldiers Who Served in Organizations from the State of Mississippi, 16th Mississippi Inf. Co. A., CSA. When Louden was arrested he said he had come to St. Louis to turn himself in.

[34] They made good use of the time Mary had another baby nine months later.

[35] NARA, RG 109, M345, roll 170; NARA, RG 94, M797, roll 40, Levi C. Turner case files. The elder Louden was reported by Federal agents to have left Richmond, made his way to Fortress Monroe, escaped from there by unknown means, returning to his home in Philadelphia November 5, 1863, where his arrival was immediately reported by agents.

[36] NARA, RG 109, M345, roll 170; Grimes was not charged with being a boat-burner. He was convicted of being a spy and mail carrier.

[37] NARA, RG 109, M345, roll 170; *St. Louis Globe-Democrat*, May 6,1888.

[38] NARA, RG 109, M345, roll 170.

[39] *OR*, Series II, Volume 7, pp. 317-21, 628-41.

[40] Grimes, 184; Headley, John W., *Confederate Operations in Canada and New York* (The Neale Publishing Company, 1906), chapter XXIII; Report of Committee of R. E. Lee Camp No. 58 U. C. V. Appointed to Investigate Charges Against Gen. Wm. H. Sebring, 1915 Florida State Archives. This latter document contains letters and statements from Young and Castleman regarding this incident, also a copy of instructions Confederate Torpedo

Bureau head, Gabriel Rains, had given to William H. Sebring as to the construction of an incendiary cartridge. Sebring adds the note that "Rains was Chief of the Secret Service of the Confederate Government, and my orders were direct from him."

41 Grimes, 189-191.

42 NARA, RG 109, M345, roll 170.

43 NARA, RG 109, M345, roll 170.

44 *St. Louis Globe-Democrat*, May 6, 1888; *OR*, Series I, Volume 48, Pt. 2, pp. 194-96; NARA, RG 109, M345, roll 97, Baker's report on Frazor.

45 NARA, RG 109, M345, roll 170, 171.

46 NARA, RG 109, M345, roll 112; Grimes, 209.

47 John Newman Edwards, *Shelby and His Men*, originally published 1867. McCoy is also credited with burning several steamboats, as well as going into St. Louis numerous times during the war with large quantities of Rebel mail.

48 *OR*, Series I, Volume 48, Pt. 2, pages 197. In this document "Judge Tucker" is Joseph W. Tucker, "John R. Barrett" is John Richard Barret, "Isaac Elshire" is probably Isaac Alshire, a steamboat mate from St. Louis.

49 William T. Sherman, *The Memoirs of General William T. Sherman by Himself* (1875).

50 NARA, RG 109, M345, roll 270, Provost Marshal's file on Joseph W. Tucker, report of Allen Pinkerton dated June 6, 1865, from New Orleans. The report by Pinkerton from his operatives and his own investigations traces Tucker leaving Mobile, Alabama in April 1865 moving northward through Grenada, Mississippi, toward Memphis. Witnesses also placed Louden in New Orleans, and possibly Mobile, during the weeks before the report.

51 Edwards, Greenough & Deved, *1866 Edward's Annual Directory*; NARA, RG 109, M345, roll 170, letter from Andrew Louden to Robert Louden, May 17, 1864.

52 Edwards, Greenough & Deved, *1867 Edward's Annual Directory*; *St. Louis Globe-Democrat*, May 6, 1888

53 Ibid.

54 *St. Louis Globe-Democrat*, May 6, 1888.

55 Ibid.

56 Quoted in: Scharf, J. Thomas, *History of the Confederate States Navy* (New York, New York, reprinted 1996 from 1887 edition), p. 762; *New York Times*, May 18, 1865.

57 Potter, 153; *Memphis Daily Bulletin*, May 2, 1865.

58 Ibid.; George Byron Merrick, *Old Times on the Upper Mississippi: The Recollections of a Steamboat Pilot from 1854 to 1863* (The Arthur H. Clark Company 1909); John Francis McDermott (ed.), *Before Mark Twain: A Sampler of Old, Old Times on the Mississippi* (Carbondale, Illinois: 1968).

59 *St. Louis Globe-Democrat*, May 6, 1888.

60 Ibid.

61 *New Orleans Times Picayune*, September 22, 1867, list of yellow fever deaths between Sept. 15 and 21, 1867. "Robert Loudon, 37, Pennsylvania." Streetor mentions his death of yellow fever in New Orleans without the date. Louden's wife remained in St. Louis until her death at age 81.

Afterword and Acknowledgements

In fall of 2005, several years after the publication of "*Sultana: A Case For Sabotage*" in *North & South Magazine*, I was contacted by the History Channel to appear in a documentary titled "Civil War Terror." This documentary still airs on various history and military channels. The focus of this documentary is the broader span of Confederate Secret Service Operations and sabotage activities in all areas of the war. As an expert in the Trans-Mississippi theater of operations, I spoke about the *Sultana* and other actions in that area. Jane Singer, a researcher of Eastern operatives and actions, was the instigator of that documentary, and I owe her great thanks for my inclusion in it.

More thanks to Jane Singer, author of *The Confederate Dirty War*, for all her generous sharing of resources and support. Historical research is often a lonely occupation and the sharing of insights and tidbits of information is done amongst many of us and is always greatly appreciated.

It was Jane who originally put me onto the *Memphis Daily Appeal* article about "Streeter" and "Lowden." Until that point, my research focus had been St. Louis, Gratiot Street Prison and its occupants (the first book I put into the works, which will be published in 2014), and the Confederate Secret

Service operatives in the Mississippi River area. When I saw the *Memphis Daily Appeal* article, standing in a bookstore holding Jerry O. Potter's *The Sultana Tragedy*, I realized I was probably the only person who knew exactly who both Streetor and Louden were, their connections, and the credibility of Streetor's story. It was then my research turned toward the *Sultana*.

Thanks to Jerry O. Potter and Gene Salecker for their marvelous research into the *Sultana* herself, and the victims and survivors of the disaster. Gene Salecker provided a great deal of material for the Boatburners section of our website at civilwarstlouis.com, and engaged us in rousing debate on issues relating to the cause of the *Sultana* disaster. In historical research and assessment, contrary viewpoints and interpretations are as important, or moreso, than agreeing viewpoints when evaluating evidence and conclusions.

Many thanks go to Keith Poulter of *North & South Magazine*. He immediately contacted me when he received my query about the original article, and his enthusiasm and professional expertise in evaluating and confirming sources never wavered from that moment until publication of the article version of *Sultana: A Case For Sabotage* in 2001.

Special thanks go to Dennis Northcott of the Missouri Historical Society in St. Louis. Dennis was our historical guide for a long time for my research into Gratiot Street Prison and the Civil War in St. Louis. It was Dennis who, on his own time, went to other archives and libraries and found the May 6, 1888 article after we explained that such an article *must* exist in St. Louis papers, and told him of its significance.

Joseph and Thomas Thatcher, descendants of Thomas Courtenay, have become valued friends, as well as generous researchers sharing their information about Courtenay and his coal torpedo. Their recent publication, *Confederate Coal Torpedo: Thomas Courtenay's Infernal Sabotage Weapon* is highly recommended.

As always in thanks and acknowledgements, many names, all valued, go without due mention. If you look at civilwarstlouis.com you will see many great authors and researchers who have contributed their work to the website and to the world. Their generous sharing is gratefully acknowledged.

The publication of this volume also owes a great deal of thanks to the PBS program *History Detectives*, and to Lion Television.

I was contacted in the spring of 2013 by *History Detectives* to appear in an episode focusing on the *Sultana*. They told me it was Jerry Potter who suggested me to them. The first shoot took place in Memphis in June 2013. I went with the production company to the field in the Mississippi River bottoms where the remains of the *Sultana* are believed to rest. It was hot, humid, and the neighboring swamp (under which one of *Sultana's* boilers rests) was full of poisonous snakes. And I wouldn't have missed it for the world!

The second interview shoot for *History Detectives* took place in August 2013 in New York City. Shortly after the interview ended, I walked a few blocks over to the World Trade Center Memorial.

Thanks always, and of course, to my husband, G. E. Rule who went from tolerating my relentless enthusiasm for Civil War research to joining in and investigating the political aspects of the Northwest Conspiracy, with his article, "The Sons of Liberty and the Louisville Warehouse Fire of July 1864" appearing in the *Lincoln Herald*. We'll be working together on a comprehensive book of the Civil War centered in St. Louis called *Spies of the Mississippi*.

D. H. Rule
August 2013

Index

Visit
variationspublishing.com
to read about upcoming
publications

and

civilwarstlouis.com

There were no good guys or bad guys,
there were only Americans fighting Americans.

to read more about
the Civil War in the west

30767051R00089